The
Grow-and-Protect
Investment
Strategy

Evidence and
Inspiration

John K. Harris, Ph.D.

Published by G&P Capital Research, LLC.
(6667 S. Jamestown Place, Tulsa OK 74136)

Outskirts Press, Inc.
http://www.outskirtspress.com

ISBN: 978-1-4787-9509-4

Library of Congress Control Number: 2017919475

Outskirts Press and the "OP" logo are trademarks belonging to Outskirts Press, Inc.

PRINTED IN THE UNITED STATES OF AMERICA

For information regarding special discounts for bulk purchases, contact:
G&P Capital Research, LLC, at John K Harris: harrisjohnk@hotmail.com

To my late friend Louise Brown who, in November 1996, provided the impetus for this book and my other investment book by asking, "Is now a good time to sell my stock funds?"

Imagine how much less stressful life would be if you could receive emails and find out whether it's considered to be timely to own or not to own stocks (the S&P 500).

Note from the Author

Contents

◇◇◇◇◇◇◇◇◇◇◇◇◇◇◇

INTRODUCTION

◇◇◇◇◇◇◇◇◇◇◇◇◇◇◇◇

I've had a lifelong interest in the stock market but never had time to study it in earnest until my retirement from being a professor at the University of Tulsa in December 1996. My study has revealed there's no better place for investors to look for guidance than the history of the stock market itself. This book takes a careful look at that history. A financial advisor can go a step further by combining the history factor and the investor's personal circumstances.

On July 20, 1997, I had what I believe was a life-changing personal spiritual experience. It concerned God and the stock market. The experience and its 20-year after-effects have moved me to write this book.

To be a successful investor—that is, being good at managing your hard-earned wealth—requires some basic knowledge such as that presented in the first five chapters of this book. Success certainly doesn't require a high IQ or special abilities. But building wealth does involve taking some risk by investing in the stock market.

This book is divided into three parts. Part One, the first two chapters, discusses the Standard and Poor's 500 Index (S&P 500)—a widely accepted benchmark of the U.S. stock market—and today's conventional investment wisdom. The conclusion from Part One is that investors would be wise to buy-and-hold the S&P 500: referred to as the "B&H strategy" throughout the book.

Part Two, Chapters 3–5, introduces and explains the brand new, proprietary grow-and-protect (G&P) strategy and sets the stage for its live test versus the B&H strategy. The test began November 2017, the month the Revised First Edition of this book was published. *Had the G&P strategy been used during the past 50 years, it would have increased returns and lowered risk compared to the B&H strategy.*

I'm optimistic about the G&P strategy competing with the B&H strategy as the future unfolds. May the better strategy win!

Part Three, Chapters 6–7, chronicles my spiritual journey mentioned above, and what I believe is God's hand in guiding my research and writing.

I wrote the book in a user-friendly style, so those less experienced can gain knowledge about investing and its terminology. To appeal to readers who are not fond of numbers, there are only five (!) presentations labeled "Table" (excluding the Appendices) that are numerical data. I think experienced investors also will find the book to be a worthwhile read.

Under the G&P strategy, an imaginary traffic signal alternates between green and red. A signal change from red to green indicates it's time to buy the S&P 500 to "grow" that portion of the investor's wealth. A signal change from green to red indicates it's time to sell the S&P 500 to "protect" that portion of the investor's wealth (that is, take a safety-first approach by trying to avoid some S&P 500 losses). Changes in the signal are emailed to those who want to receive them. To be included in my free email distributions, send me an email: harrisjohnk@hotmail.com

For 1966–2015 (the 50-year period covered in the book), the traffic signal was red 18% of the time. Not holding the S&P 500 during the red-signal times held the G&P investor's wealth steady, thereby eliminating stock market risk. Because human nature never changes, the emotions of greed, hope, fear and regret affected the buying and selling of stocks at any time in the past just as much as they do now.

Evidence of my credentials as a stock market historian can be seen in the citations to my research in *Barron's,* the weekly Dow Jones newspaper, which appear in Table D-3 (p. 110). Moreover, I have a Ph.D. in accounting, was a CPA for 30 years and authored (also for 30 years) the popular *Student Guide* that accompanied the world's leading textbook in its field, Charles T. Horngren, Srikant M. Datar and Madhav V. Rajan's *Cost Accounting: A Managerial Emphasis*—now in its 16th edition.

John K. Harris
Tulsa, OK
October 14, 2016

Revised First Edition (RFE)

Compared to the original version of this book (published October 16, 2016), the RFE (published November 26, 2017) incorporates four changes:

1. The companion website for the original version is no more; it has been replaced by my free email distributions. If you're not included in the distributions but want to be, send me an email:

harrisjohnk@hotmail.com

2. Typos found—less than a dozen of them—have been corrected. If you find a typo(s), please let me know.

3. Changes have been made to add clarity. If you see the need for more of this type of change, please let me know.

4. Appendices G and H are new. I suggest you read the **G&P** Orientation (pp. 132–134) in Appendix G at this time.

In my opinion, the RFE is much improved compared to the original version. I hope you enjoy reading this unconventional, highly eclectic book: that is, Parts One and Two sharply contrast with Part Three.

Feedback from readers is welcome.

Reflections

As this Revised First Edition goes to press, I have these reflections.

Almost all of today's leading academic scholars and luminaries, such as Warren Buffett and Vanguard's founder John Bogle, maintain that market timing can't be done profitably in a consistent manner. According to that view, *market timing is a fool's errand*. That mighty conclusion is examined in Part Two (pp. 33–57) and Appendix H (pp. 143–146).

I'm reminded of these excerpts from David McCullough's 2005 book, *The Wright Brothers*:

p. 1:   "From ancient times and into the Middle Ages, man had dreamed of taking to the sky, of soaring into the blue like birds. One savant in Spain in the year 875 is known to have covered himself with feathers in an attempt. Others devised wings of their own design and jumped from rooftops and towers—some to their deaths."

p. 28: "Otto Lilienthal, a German glider enthusiast who designed and built more than a dozen different gliders, died in a glider accident in 1896."

p. 33: "[The Wright brothers faced the ever-present] risks of humiliating failure."

p. 34: "On December 24, 1897, the *Washington Post* categorically declared, 'It is a fact that man can't fly.'"

p. 63: "Wilbur [Wright] was at such a low point at Kitty Hawk [North Carolina] in Fall 1901 that he declared, 'not in a thousand years would man ever fly.'"

p. 69: "An article in the September 1901 issue of the popular *McClure's Magazine* written by Simon Newcomb, a distinguished astronomer and professor at Johns Hopkins University, discussed the dream of human flight as no more than a myth."

Then, finally success came. Human flight was possible and practical: (https://airandspace.si.edu/exhibitions/wright-brothers/online/)

"On December 17, 1903, Wilbur and Orville Wright made four brief flights at Kitty Hawk with their first powered aircraft. The Wright brothers had invented the first successful airplane."

Now returning to the topic of market timing. In general, efforts at market timing have been colossal failures. You have in hand the book that describes the grow-and-protect (G&P) model for market timing. So now, let the future performance of the G&P model (for 2018, 2019...) be what it may be vs. the B&H model. Time will tell which model is better.

Obviously, I would not have included this section on my reflections unless I am confident that the G&P model will outperform B&H as the future unfolds.

John K. Harris
Tulsa, OK
November 26, 2017

John K. Harris, Ph.D.
Stock market historian
harrisjohnk@hotmail.com

author: **The *Grow*-and-*Protect* Investment Strategy:** *Evidence and Inspiration*

Professor Emeritus, University of Tulsa

ACKNOWLEDGEMENTS

◇◇◇◇◇◇◇◇◇◇◇◇◇◇◇◇

First and foremost, I thank God for blessing me with the ability and opportunity to write this book, which I present to His glory.

I thank my research partner, Kip Karney, who by profession is a microbiologist. A mutual respect for stock market history has fueled our 18-year quest, which resulted in the grow-and-protect (G&P) investment strategy. Our research has been on-going at widely varying paces.

I thank my reviewers—all friends—for their comments: Kip Karney, Charlie Bennett, Del Chesser, Bruce Clutter, Nancy Goodman, Lisa Hanold, John Lenschow, Pat Lloyd, Charles Long, Frank McDaniel, Mike Moran, Gerald Rathjen, Eric Samuelson, Doug Scott, Pierre Smith and Philip Viles.

I thank Jim Payne for teaching me to use Microsoft Excel. He is an outstanding teacher!

Whether they knew it or not, several hundred people have been a part of my spiritual journey related to this book; see Part Two (pp. 59–78). If you are one of them, you can see where you plug in. I thank all of you.

I thank my wife Judith for her love, assistance and patience throughout the many years of my research and writing. I'm particularly grateful she gave me permission to write this book.

PART ONE

Investing in the S&P 500: The Buy-and-Hold (B&H) Strategy

Chapter 1 is a "really get familiar" look at the S&P 500 Index. Facts about the S&P 500's returns and risk are informative to investors. History, which tells everything that's known about the S&P 500, is the basis of the widely used buy-and-hold (B&H) strategy. The S&P 500 investor's performance has been enhanced by the advent of low-cost index funds and exchange-traded funds.

Today's conventional investment wisdom (Chapter 2) is based on modern portfolio theory; its early development was done by many scholars who won the Nobel Prize in Economics. Two of the main tenets of modern portfolio theory are asset allocation and the efficient market theory. The efficient market theory is emphatic that investors should use the B&H strategy.

Chapters 1 and 2 present a strong argument for investors to accumulate wealth by using the B&H strategy.

Chapter 1

◇◇◇◇◇◇◇◇◇◇◇◇◇◇◇◇◇

The S&P 500

Chapter Overview

This chapter takes a close look at the Standard and Poor's 500 Index (S&P 500), the U.S.'s premier stock market index. The two measures of the S&P 500's performance are return and risk. For the 1966–2015 period (50 years), the S&P 500's average (mean) annual return was 11%. The Index's historically generous return went hand-in-hand with considerable risk, which is seen in severe declines in the S&P 500 from time to time—such as the 57% decline in the 17 months ended March 9, 2009.

History has played the important role in developing the popular **buy**-and-hold (**B&H**) strategy for investing in the S&P 500. There are significant benefits of **buy**ing-and-holding low-cost S&P 500 index funds, including low capital gains due to low turnover.

The **S&P 500** is broad-based, comprised of 500 of the largest companies headquartered in the U.S.[1]—including General Electric, Bank of America, Microsoft, Apple, ExxonMobil, UnitedHealth Group, Facebook, Johnson & Johnson, McDonalds, Nike, Coca-Cola, IBM, Home Depot, Boeing, Verizon, Starbucks, Wal-Mart, Amazon, Walt Disney and some many of us have probably never heard of. The 500 companies are selected by the S&P Index Committee, a team of analysts and economists at Standard and Poor's.

The S&P 500 represents about 80% of the total market value of all publicly traded U.S. stocks and some 40% of the total market value of all publicly traded stocks in the entire world. As a group, the 500 companies have a massive global reach: They derive about one-third of their sales abroad. Over

---

1 In this book, "Important Terms to Know" appear in bold-faced type where they are defined. The S&P 500 is the first of these terms. All the Important Terms to Know comprise the Glossary at the end of the book.

the past 20 years, the S&P 500 outperformed all other major world stock indexes when risk is taken into account.

Of course, to invest in the S&P 500 or anywhere else in the financial markets, you need money. If you're fortunate, you have inherited (or will inherit) money for investing. The other main source of money for investing is savings. Saving is putting money away; investing is putting money to work. Appendix A (pp. 79–81) discusses Saving for Retirement.[2]

The current price of the S&P 500 is prominently displayed on financial cable channels. If you belong to a health club, you've likely noticed the S&P 500 on TV there. Of course, the S&P 500 is tracked in newspapers and on the Internet.

The S&P 500 is a widely-used barometer of the U.S. stock market. It's the benchmark for evaluating the performance of many institutional investors and professional money managers. The S&P 500 is weighted by each company's total market value. For example, Apple is weighted almost four times as much as Disney.

All 30 stocks in the Dow Jones Industrial Average (the Dow) are in the S&P 500, so the Dow—the oldest U.S. stock index and best known among many investors—is a subset of the S&P 500. Other than the S&P 500 (large caps), the main segments of the U.S. stock market are small companies (small caps) and mid-sized companies (mid caps). Foreign stocks are another important market segment. Segments of the stock market other than the S&P 500 are beyond the scope of this book.

The S&P Composite Index was launched on a daily basis at the beginning of 1928 (then only 90 stocks, which was expanded to 500 stocks in 1957), so it is almost 90 years old. To simplify my presentation, the book focuses on the last 50 years of the S&P 500's life (1966–2015). Because human nature never changes, the emotions of greed, hope, fear and regret affected the buying and selling of stocks at any time in the past just as much as they do now.

The S&P 500 has been updated from time to time by adding companies that meet Standard & Poor's criteria for total market value, earnings and liquidity while deleting an equal number that fail to meet the criteria.[3]

Consider this example about the S&P 500. On July 28, 2016 (the day I wrote this paragraph), the S&P 500's closing price was 2170.06. The previous day's closing price was 2166.58. It is simple and interesting to think of each trading day in this way. All the day's news—economic, geopolitical and so on—is poured into the top of an imaginary "investor perception-and-interpretation

---

2   This is the first of the book's eight Appendices. *Each of them is optional.* If the subject is not of interest to you, skip that Appendix.

3   Jeremy J. Siegel, *Stocks for the Long Run*, 4th edition (McGraw Hill, 2008), p. 52.

funnel" and out the bottom comes the day's S&P 500 closing price. The change in the daily closing price reflects investors' sentiment about (reaction to) the day's news. It's truly fascinating to see this gigantic flow of daily information processed by millions of investors. On July 28, 2016, the S&P 500 rose a modest 0.16% [(2170.06/2166.58) − 1]. I don't know the requirements for something to be a Wonder of the World, but in my mind the S&P 500 is one.

Interestingly, economic news and geopolitical news often affect the S&P 500 in different ways, at different times and in different economic cycles. Because of these differences, the S&P 500's movements are a mystery to many investors much of the time. Here's a colorful description of the situation:[4]

> "When investors feel upbeat, they focus on the news that supports a rosy outlook. If sentiment is negative, they see the glass half-empty and look for cracks."

It was clear why the S&P 500 fell sharply immediately after the 9/11 terrorist attacks. However, it may surprise most investors that in the vast majority of cases, major movements in the S&P 500 are *not* accompanied by any news that explains why they occurred. In fact, less than 1 in 4 major moves in the S&P 500 can be clearly linked to a specific world economic or geopolitical event.[5] This confirms the unpredictability of the stock market (the S&P 500) and the difficulty in forecasting market moves.[6]

As a current example, consider 2016 at the end of July. According to the front page of *The Wall Street Journal* on July 30–31, the Commerce Department reported that U.S. economic growth is now tracking at an unusually slow 1% rate in 2016. Meanwhile, the S&P 500 (including reinvested dividends) is up 7.7% year-to-date, following the worst six-week start of any year in history! Confusing, isn't it?

Getting Your Investing Job Done

Many individual investors prefer to do most or all the work of investing themselves, whereas others rely on financial advisers. For each investor, that choice depends on five main factors: (1) knowledge of investing, (2) inclination to actually do the work involved in investing, (3) time available for investing, (4) patience and discipline and (5) self-confidence. In addition, prudent investors should do a good job in controlling the costs (fees) associated with investing—including (if applicable) the cost of having a financial adviser. All these factors are addressed at various places in the book.

4   Scott Patterson, *The Wall Street Journal* (January 23, 2007), p. C1.
5   Jeremy J. Siegel, *Stocks for the Long Run*, 4th edition (McGraw Hill, 2008), p. 223.
6   Jeremy J. Siegel, *Stocks for the Long Run*, 4th edition (McGraw Hill, 2008), p. 235.

It is important to put the S&P 500 in perspective in regard to your asset allocation. Generally speaking, asset allocation refers to deciding on and maintaining a suitable mix of stocks, bonds, and cash equivalents in your portfolio as you move through the seasons of life. Your portfolio encompasses all of your 401(k), IRA and taxable accounts. The S&P 500 (or a representative large-cap fund) should be a core holding in your portfolio. Personally, I would be totally comfortable having the S&P 500 as the entire stock portion of my portfolio; I think you'll understand why later in this chapter and the next.

S&P 500 Returns for 1966–2015

The **S&P 500's annual return** is the sum of its price change and the companies' cash dividends paid to investors (the **dividend yield**), expressed as a percentage of its beginning-of-the-year price. Let's use 2015 as an example. At the end of 2014, the S&P 500 was 2058.90. It fell to 2043.94 at the end of 2015, so the price declined 0.73% [(2043.94/2058.90) − 1]. 2015 had a dividend yield of 2.02%. So,

$$\text{2015's return} = -0.73\% + 2.02\% = 1.29\%$$

For 2015, the S&P 500's price change was negative but, because of the dividend yield being larger, the return was positive.

For 1966–2015, the S&P 500's dividend yield ranged from 1.04% for 2000 to 6.65% for 1982. The dividend yield plays a bigger role in the total accumulation of a long-term investment in the S&P 500 than you might think. Consider a $1,000 investment in the S&P 500 at the beginning of 1966, which was held until the end of 2015. The total accumulation *without* dividends would have been $22,112. The total accumulation *with* dividends reinvested would have been $101,354. The difference is $79,242! That extraordinarily large amount is due to the magic of compounding the annual dividends.

Chart 1-1 shows the S&P 500 annual returns for 1966–2015 (50 years). The returns fluctuated widely above and below their average (mean) of 11%[7] and appear to be random. In fact, the correlation between the S&P 500's return in a given year and its return for the preceding year is virtually zero.

---

7   The sum of all 50 annual returns divided by 50.

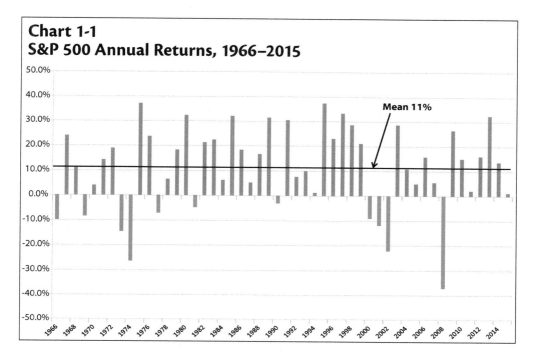

Chart 1-1
S&P 500 Annual Returns, 1966–2015

The 11% mean annual return far exceeded the mean annual rate of inflation, which was about 4¼%. The annual excess of return over inflation was about 7%.

Consider two asset classes: the S&P 500 and bonds.[8] Bonds' long-term mean annual return is 7.8%. Bonds are less volatile than stocks, and they generally have a low correlation. In choosing the mix of the two asset classes, the investor shouldn't be overly cautious about the S&P 500 portion of his portfolio. Being unafraid of the stock market is a life skill that many investors have never learned.

Table 1-1, column (2), presents the S&P 500 annual returns for 1966–2015, with the mean of 11% on the bottom line. Column (3) flags the years that had negative returns: 11 of the 50 years had negative returns—none since 2008.

---

8   Throughout the body of the book, only those two asset classes are used. Appendix B on Asset Allocation will relax this restriction.

Table 1-1[9]
S&P 500 Annual Returns, 1966–2015

Year (1)	S&P 500 Return (2)	Negative Return (3)	Year (1)	S&P 500 Return (2)	Negative Return (3)
1966	−10%	◄	1991	31%	
1967	24%		1992	8%	
1968	11%		1993	10%	
1969	−9%	◄	1994	1%	
1970	4%		1995	37%	
1971	14%		1996	23%	
1972	19%		1997	33%	
1973	−15%	◄	1998	29%	
1974	−26%	◄	1999	21%	
1975	37%		2000	−9%	◄
1976	24%		2001	−12%	◄
1977	−7%	◄	2002	−22%	◄
1978	7%		2003	29%	
1979	18%		2004	11%	
1980	32%		2005	5%	
1981	−5%	◄	2006	16%	
1982	21%		2007	5%	
1983	23%		2008	−37%	◄
1984	6%		2009	26%	
1985	32%		2010	15%	
1986	18%		2011	2%	
1987	5%		2012	16%	
1988	17%		2013	32%	
1989	31%		2014	14%	
1990	−3%	◄	2015	1%	
			Mean	11%	

These negative returns introduce the concept of risk, which is discussed in the next section.

Despite the negative returns, a $1,000 investment made at the beginning of each of the five 10-year periods in the table resulted in desirable total accumulations for that 10-year period:

1966–1975	$1,380
1976–1985	$3,816
1986–1995	$3,991
1996–2005	$2,385
2006–2015	$2,022

9   This is the first of only five full-fledged numerical tables in the body of the book. As a result, I suggest you spend a few minutes studying the table.

S&P 500 Risk for 1966–2015

The **S&P 500's risk** is the uncertainty of its future market price. In the practical application of this definition of risk, investors owning the S&P 500 mainly concern themselves with the possibility of the S&P 500 declining in market price. Although investing in the S&P 500 is quite risky, disciplined investors have the confidence and perspective to endure the S&P 500's inevitable declines, because of the long-term mean annual return of 11%.

Many investors unwisely focus on investment returns while paying less attention to risk. No investment strategy can be adequately judged without considering both return and risk.

Although most investors express a strong distaste for significant market declines, such volatility must be accepted in order to reap the superior returns offered by the S&P 500. For risk is the essence of the S&P 500's sizable returns. Investors cannot make any more than the risk-free rate of return on short-term U.S. Treasury bills unless there is some possibility that they can make less.[10]

There are two simple but useful measures of the S&P 500's risk: (1) its largest declines and (2) the minimum number of calendar years needed to recoup the maximum loss. Here are the six largest year-to-date (YTD) declines (listed by size) paired with the corresponding annual returns:

Date	Maximum YTD Decline	Annual Return
11/20/08	−49%	−37%
10/03/74	−36%	−26%
10/09/02	−32%	−22%
09/21/01	−27%	−12%
03/09/09	−25%	**26%**
05/26/70	−25%	**4%**

The returns for 2009 and 1970 are in bold because they were positive, despite the severe declines *within* each of these years. No wonder many people are hesitant to invest heavily in the stock market.

The full lengths of the worst bear markets[11] during 1966–2015 were much more severe:

Bear market began	Bear market ended	Months	S&P 500 change
10/09/07	03/09/09	17.0	−57%
03/24/00	10/09/02	30.5	−49%
01/11/73	10/03/74	20.7	−48%

10 Jeremy J. Siegel, *Stocks for the Long Run*, 4th edition (McGraw Hill, 2008), p. 277.

11 A bear market occurs when the S&P 500 declines 20% or more.

"If you think [S&P 500] can't fall by at least 50% again, you are wrong."[12]

When experienced investors endure such large declines in the S&P 500 several times over a few decades, they know it's different verses of the same market song. In this regard, a mutual fund executive made this astute observation in the summer of 2001 when the S&P 500 was in the midst of a large decline, which got much worse immediately after 9/11:

> "While every period of market volatility occurs in a different way and typically for different reasons, there is often a feeling of déjà vu associated with market fluctuations."[13]

The second measure of risk is the minimum number of calendar years needed to avoid a loss while owning the S&P 500. Table 1-2, column (3), indicates 7 calendar years are required to avoid virtually all losses—the 7-calendar-year mean annual return for 1960–1966, 1961–1967...and 2009–2015. With the exception of the tiny negative 0.2% mean annual return for 1968–1974, all of the 7-year means were positive.

---

12 Jason Zweig, *The Wall Street Journal* (August 15–16, 2015), p. C1.

13 Mark H. Williamson, Invesco newsletter (Summer 2001), p. 2.

Table 1-2
S&P 500 7-Calendar-Year Mean Annual Returns, 1966–2015

Year (1)	S&P 500 Return (2)	7-Calendar-Year Mean Annual Return (3)	Year (1)	S&P 500 Return (2)	7-Calendar-Year Mean Annual Return (3)
1960	0%		1988	17%	18%
1961	27%		1989	31%	19%
1962	−9%		1990	−3%	15%
1963	23%		1991	31%	19%
1964	16%		1992	8%	15%
1965	12%		1993	10%	14%
1966	−10%	9%	1994	1%	14%
1967	24%	12%	1995	37%	16%
1968	11%	10%	1996	23%	15%
1969	−9%	10%	1997	33%	20%
1970	4%	7%	1998	29%	20%
1971	14%	7%	1999	21%	22%
1972	19%	8%	2000	−9%	19%
1973	−15%	7%	2001	−12%	17%
1974	−26%	−0.2%	2002	−22%	9%
1975	37%	4%	2003	29%	10%
1976	24%	8%	2004	11%	7%
1977	−7%	7%	2005	5%	3%
1978	7%	5%	2006	16%	2%
1979	18%	5%	2007	5%	5%
1980	32%	12%	2008	−37%	1%
1981	−5%	15%	2009	26%	8%
1982	21%	13%	2010	15%	6%
1983	23%	13%	2011	2%	5%
1984	6%	15%	2012	16%	6%
1985	32%	18%	2013	32%	9%
1986	18%	18%	2014	14%	10%
1987	5%	14%	2015	1%	15%

Reversion to the Mean

The 7-calendar-year mean annual return introduces the fact that there is an immutable force affecting the S&P 500 (and at work in all financial markets), which is borne out by history. It is called **reversion to the mean**. Under this force, periods of high returns tend to occur after periods of lower returns, and in turn, periods of low returns tend to follow periods of higher returns. As a result, the S&P 500 returns over, say, any 20-year period tend to have a mean that is nearly the same as the long-term mean of 11%. The S&P 500's mean annual return for two 20-year periods illustrates reversion to the mean:

20-Year Period	Mean Annual Return
1966–1985	10%
1994–2013	11%

History Tells Investors Everything That's Known[14]

In talking with many people near my age (I'm 76), they say: "The older they get, the more appreciation they have for history." I feel that same way. Beyond mere appreciation for the S&P 500's history lessons in this chapter, what role does history play?

History clearly shows that there is a tradeoff between the S&P 500's risk and its return. In fact, 15 times since 1966, the S&P 500 has declined by 19% to as much as 57%. However from the beginning of 1966 to the end of 2015, the S&P 500 rose 21,113% [(2043.94/92.43)−1]—reflecting the fantastic performance of the greatest economy in the world.

Suppose you came to the U.S. from Mars and got a job. One of the fringe benefits of your job is a 401(k). But being from Mars, you know absolutely nothing about investing. How would you decide what to invest in? Well, you'd probably look at material about the 401(k) plan supplied by the Human Resources department, and might attend a meeting to help employees make wise decisions about what type of investments to include in their 401(k)s. Assume you're instructed that those decisions should be based on your age and your attitude toward risk. The history of what has happened to stocks and bonds over the years provides good guidance for your decisions.

Here's what two renowned writers believe about history:

◆ "Thoughtful, objective study of the past is the best (and also the least costly) way to develop an understanding of the basic nature of investments and [financial] markets."[15]

---

14 As you read this section, keep in mind the popular humorist maxim, which is attributed to Mark Twain: "History doesn't repeat itself, but it often rhymes."

15 Charles D. Ellis, *Winning the Loser's Game*, 4th edition (McGraw Hill, 2002), p. 86.

◆ "Although there is no guarantee that ... patterns of the past, no matter how deeply ingrained in the historical record, will prevail in the future, a study of the past, accompanied by a self-administered dose of common sense, is the intelligent investor's best recourse."[16]

People have nowhere else to look for investment guidance except history— whether they find it in their own searches or learn it from mutual fund literature and/or financial advisers. The bottom line is that human nature (see p. 70) is the dominant factor in the historical movements of the S&P 500.

The Buy-and-Hold (B&H) Strategy

Data mining is searching historical data for patterns that repeat themselves with a high degree of consistency.[17] Data mining is facilitated by computing power becoming so inexpensive.[18] The often-heard quip about data mining is: "Torture the data enough, and it will confess [that is, a new market-timing strategy will be born]!" This chapter's discussion of the S&P 500's return and risk profile is an example of data mining. We saw that, despite some very severe declines over the years, the S&P 500 had a highly desirable mean annual return of 11% for 1966–2015. Recall from earlier in the chapter, a $1,000 investment in the S&P 500 at the beginning of 1966 with dividends reinvested would have produced a total accumulation at the end of 2015 of $101,354.

We also saw that the immutable principle of reversion to the mean was at work in 1966–2015. The example I used spanned two 20-year periods: 1966–1985 and 1994–2013. But what about 20-year periods *before* 1966? Recall that the S&P 500 was launched on a daily basis at the beginning of 1928 (then only 90 stocks). The mean annual return for the 20 year period of 1928–1947—a time that included the generally poor returns of the Great Depression—was 8%. The mean annual return for the 20-year period, 1946–1965, was 15%.

So, data mining the S&P 500 during 1928–2015 has produced what is called the **buy-and-hold (B&H) strategy**. Here is another quote from the legendary John Bogle, founder of the Vanguard Group:[19]

> "The stock and bond markets are unpredictable on a short-term basis, but their long-term patterns of risk and return have proved durable enough to serve as the basis of a long-term [B&H] strategy that leads to investment success."

16 John C. Bogle, *Common Sense on Mutual Funds* (Wiley, 1999), p. 6.

17 For an academic article on data mining, see Andrew Lo and Craig MacKinlay, "Data-Snooping Biases in Tests of Financial Asset Pricing Models," *Review of Financial Studies* (Fall 1999), pp. 431–467.

18 Jeremy J. Siegel, *Stocks for the Long Run*, 4th edition (McGraw Hill, 2008), pp. 326–327.

19   John C. Bogle, *Common Sense on Mutual Funds* (Wiley, 1999), p. 6.

I think it's accurate to say there is no stronger advocate of the B&H strategy than John Bogle.

An important practical aspect of the B&H strategy[20] is that anyone can be as good as the average investor *with no practice at all*. That's clearly a wonderful exception to the general rule that most of us have no chance of being as good as average in a pursuit that others practice for years to hone their skills.[21]

Strong advocates of the B&H strategy are too numerous to count. You probably have heard the B&H mantra from mutual-fund companies and/or a financial adviser.

Millions of investors steadfastly use the B&H strategy with a sizable representation of the S&P 500 included in their portfolios. Generally, this strategy is combined with **dollar-cost averaging**. Dollar-cost averaging is investing a set amount of money at regular intervals, such as making monthly contributions to your 401(k). For these investors to even consider abandoning the B&H strategy (coupled with dollar-cost averaging) is completely out of the question. This attitude has led to the widely-held view that investment success over the long term is a function of *time in the market* rather than *market timing*. The importance of financial-market history strikes again.

To be successful using the B&H strategy, investors must control their emotions and not sell—as they inevitably become aware of the down movements of the S&P 500—and let their reason prevail over the long term.[22] However, this formula for success is much easier said than done, primarily because there is a strong tendency for investors' emotions to overpower their intellects. Financial advisors can help investors control their emotions.

Financial News

The critical question is, will the investor use the B&H strategy for the long term, so the expected mean annual return will be achieved?[23] Investors' emotions often move contrary to their rational economic interests.[24] And that's where emotionally-stimulating financial news can come into play.

People often make investment decisions based on their emotions when a cool, rational analysis would call for very different actions.[25] B&H investors have the option to *completely ignore financial news*, if that's even possible in

---

20 To simplify the exposition henceforth in the book, "B&H strategy" will be used instead of the cumbersome phrase "B&H strategy for the S&P 500." In cases where the B&H strategy refers to non-S&P 500 assets, that will be specified.

21 Jeremy J. Siegel, *Stocks for the Long Run*, 4th edition (McGraw Hill, 2008), p. 342.

22 John C. Bogle, *Bogle on Mutual Funds* (Irwin, 1994), p. 61.

23 Charles D. Ellis, *Winning the Loser's Game*, 4th edition (McGraw Hill, 2002), p. 42.

24 Charles D. Ellis, *Winning the Loser's Game*, 4th edition (McGraw Hill, 2002), p. 138.

25 Charles D. Ellis, *Winning the Loser's Game*, 4th edition (McGraw Hill, 2002), p. 84.

today's world. The potential danger of keeping up with the financial news is that it can be emotionally stimulating. Of course, B&H investors should not let their emotions interfere with their staunch, stay-the-course approach. As a practical matter, financial news can be interesting, educational, intellectually stimulating and entertaining.

I read an Internet article in early July 2016, titled "Five Things to Know About Brexit." I think it was interesting, educational and intellectually stimulating.

In terms of entertainment, almost every month I watch the release of the employment report on CNBC, usually the first Friday of the month at 8:30 am Eastern time. I indulge myself for about 20 minutes, 10 minutes before the release of the actual jobs number and 10 minutes after. A panel of five or so experts give their estimates regarding the number of jobs created the previous month. Often the estimates vary widely. Some months one or more estimates are close to the actual number of jobs created. Other months none of the experts are even close to the actual number. Not only is it entertaining for me to see how close the panelists' estimates are to the actual number, but I like to watch the up and down movements of the S&P futures during the 20-minute span. Oftentimes, the real S&P fireworks occur seconds after the jobs number is released.

Millions of investors watch the intra-day movements in the S&P 500 and its closing prices—that's financial news. Include me in that group. This activity is somewhat like watching the movement of the ball at a soccer match. If you find it interesting, there's nothing wrong with following the S&P 500's bouncing ball.

Low-Cost S&P 500 Index Funds

In today's investment world, the only prudent way to implement the B&H strategy is via low-cost **S&P 500 index funds**. These funds are passively-managed so they mimic the S&P 500's return. They have low turnover because the S&P 500 companies change infrequently, thereby leading to low trading costs and low capital gains. *A low-cost S&P 500 index fund outperforms the vast majority of professional money managers in most years.*

There are two types of index funds: mutual funds and **exchange-traded funds (ETFs)**. The mutual funds are priced once a day when the financial markets close at 4 pm Eastern time. Mutual fund companies charge a redemption fee if their funds are held for less than 90 days. ETFs trade all day like stocks. To trade ETFs, it's necessary to have a brokerage account—whether for a 401(k), IRA or taxable account—that allows those trades. S&P 500 index mutual funds and S&P 500 ETFs were launched in 1976 and 1993, respectively.

All investors should give a big tip-of-the-cap to the visionary, John Bogle, who made the Vanguard 500 Index Fund available to individual investors in August 1976. This 40-year-old fund is now the largest mutual fund on the planet. *In my opinion, John Bogle deserves a Presidential Medal of Freedom, a Congressional Gold Medal and/or a Nobel Prize in Economics for his excellent innovation that has benefited many millions of investors.*

Table 1-3 lists leading low-cost S&P 500 index funds that are well suited for the B&H strategy. All these funds did and do an excellent low-cost job of mimicking the S&P 500 return. Be aware that an expense ratio of only 0.09% (plus a tiny amount of tracking error) means that *the total cost to invest $10,000 is less than four pennies per trading day!* And portfolio turnover is very low, so there are almost no trading costs. Both Fidelity and Vanguard offer even lower-cost index funds to investors who have a fund balance of $10,000 or more.

Table 1-3
Low-Cost S&P 500 Index Funds

Mutual Fund	Ticker Symbol	Annual Expense Ratio	Minimum Investment
Fidelity 500 Index Fund (investor class)	FUSEX	0.09%	$2,500
Fidelity 500 Index Fund (premium class)	FUSVX	0.045%	$10,000
Schwab S&P 500 Index Fund	SWPPX	0.09%	$100
Vanguard 500 Index Fund (investor class)	VFINX	0.16%	$3,000
Vanguard 500 Index Fund (Admiral class)	VFIAX	0.05%	$10,000
Vanguard 500 Index Fund (institutional class)	VINIX	0.04%	$5 million
Vanguard 500 Index Fund (institutional-plus class)	VIIIX	0.02%	$200 million
Vanguard 500 Index Fund (select class)	VFFSX	0.01%	$5 billion
Exchange-Traded Fund (ETF)			
iShares Core S&P 500	IVV	0.04%	None
Standard & Poor's Depository Receipts S&P 500 (called "Spiders")	SPY	0.09%	None
Vanguard 500 Index	VOO	0.05%	None

Be aware that all S&P 500 index mutual funds are not created equal. Almost all of these funds charge much higher annual investment costs than the funds listed in Table 1-3. In fact, on average for 2015, S&P 500 index mutual funds had an annual expense ratio greater than 0.50%. Also in 2015, some 20 S&P 500 index mutual funds had expense ratios in excess of 1.20%!

Actively-Managed Mutual Funds

In contrast to passively-managed mutual funds, **actively-managed mutual funds** are managed by professional money managers who engage in stock picking or market timing in an effort to outperform a benchmark index such as the S&P 500. Actively-managed funds charge high annual fees—and some have a front-end sales charge (a load) too. The higher fund fees are the kiss of death for investors! These fees are a major reason why active funds have significantly underperformed passive funds for most years.[26] It's really no contest. As a result in today's world, 401(k)-type plans should use index funds rather than actively-managed funds. Unfortunately, many companies have not yet included index funds in their 401(k) plans.

> Recall that for 1966–2015, the S&P 500 mean annual return was 11%. Investing $1,000 and letting it grow at 11% per year for a 30-year period would produce a total accumulation of almost $22,900. Incurring a 1% annual investment fee—thereby lowering the annual return to 10%—would reduce the final accumulation by almost 25%. For the investor to be as well off economically, incurring that 1% annual fee would require him to retire two years later than if there was no fee. (Note that financial advisers typically charge a 1% fee based on the client's account balance.)
>
> Consider another example that highlights the importance of investment fees. Assume you invest $1,000 and earn a gross annual return of 11%. The total accumulations from that investment under two contrasting fee schedules are as follows:
>
> | Years After Initial Investment | Account Balance 0.1% Annual Fee | 1.5% Annual Fee | Benefit of Lower Fee |
> |---|---|---|---|
> | 10 | $2,814 | $2,478 | 12% |
> | 20 | $7,918 | $6,142 | 22% |
> | 30 | $22,282 | $15,220 | 32% |

---

26 The other main reasons for their underperformance are poor stock picking and poor market timing.

> In light of these examples, it's a good idea for you to *check the fees you are incurring for each fund you own—* whether in your 401(k), IRA or taxable account. Google each fund's name and get the ticker symbol. Then, go to morningstar.com and enter the ticker symbol. Look for the fund's annual expense ratio, which gives you an estimate of its fees. Note that the annual expense ratio does not include trading costs, which often exceed 0.50% per year.

A recent article[27] reported that the investing public is increasingly looking askance at portfolio managers who are paid handsome salaries but deliver mediocre performance. The trend is seen in the mass investor exodus from actively-managed funds to passive index funds and exchange-traded funds. *The Wall Street Journal* reported the trend is likely to be accelerated by new fiduciary rules for financial advisers.[28]

According to Morningstar, there was a swing of over $1 trillion from 2009 through mid-2016. While actively managed mutual funds lost $728.9 billion in assets, ETFs gained $342.8 billion. Investors pulled $317 billion from actively managed funds over the year ending June 30, 2016, while pouring $373.3 billion into passive funds.[29] According to Morgan Stanley, growth in assets under management for the fund industry as a whole, has been 0.9% over the first seven months of 2016, but ETF growth was a much faster 8.9%.[30] In other words, investors (and their advisers) have become aggressively passive.

Not Investing in Low-Cost S&P 500 Index Funds

Despite the facts presented above, millions of people invest in stock funds that are not low-cost S&P 500 index funds. The alternatives include:

◆ Higher-cost S&P 500 index funds

◆ Higher-cost non-S&P 500 stock index funds (small caps, mid caps, REITs and foreign stocks)

◆ Higher-cost actively-managed stock mutual funds

Why would an investor choose a higher-cost S&P 500 index fund instead of a low-cost S&P 500 index fund? Three reasons: (1) that's his only S&P 500

---

27 Randall W. Forsyth, *Barron's* (August 15, 2016), p. 6.

28 *The Wall Street Journal* (August 16, 2016), p. C8.

29 *The Wall Street Journal* (August 12, 2016), p. C1.

30 *The Wall Street Journal* (August 16, 2016), p. C8.

choice in the 401(k) plan, (2) sentiment or (3) a lack of investment knowledge. Regarding sentiment, a widow might **buy** a higher-cost S&P 500 index fund at her late husband's bank—rarely, but sometimes with a load fee—because he liked the bank. Hopefully, this chapter enlightens her as well as those who previously lacked the knowledge about low-cost S&P 500 funds.

Buying non-S&P 500 index funds would improve your portfolio's diversification in stocks. But you can simplify your portfolio and **buy** a low-cost S&P 500 index fund.

What about the alternative of actively-managed stock mutual funds? It's a shame when these funds are the only type of stock fund available in a 401(k) plan, since as noted above, in most years they underperform the S&P 500. In February, 2016, the financial press reported, for the 10-year period 2006–2015, only 18% of all large-cap U.S. stock mutual funds outperformed the S&P 500. The burden of high fees (for example, salaries of professional money managers and advertising) is a main reason 82% of these funds underperformed the S&P 500. For most 10 year periods, the odds have been about 1 in 5 of an actively-managed fund beating a low-cost S&P 500 index fund. I expect similar odds will prevail for 2016–2025. Are you feeling lucky?

Recent Litigation[31]

The Massachusetts Institute of Technology, New York University and Yale University were sued August 9, 2016 for allegedly causing participants in their retirement-savings plans to pay excessive fees, making them the latest to be targeted in a wave of similar litigation challenging the use of retail mutual funds [including actively-managed funds with poor track records] in 401(k) and other retirement plans.

As with many of the previous 401(k) fee cases, the new suits allege the plans breached their duties under the Employee Retirement Income Security Act of 1974 by stocking their investments with retail mutual funds rather than lower-cost institutional versions of the same investments.

With billions of dollars in assets, the plans have the "bargaining power" to secure lower fee investment products, said Jerome Schlichter, whose St. Louis law firm, Schlichter, Bogard & Denton, filed the cases. "These universities don't have retail mutual funds in their endowments. Our position is that a multibillion-dollar 403(b) or 401(k) plan shouldn't have them in a retirement plan either."

The suits come on the heels of several others that have been filed in recent weeks against companies, including financial-services firms, which have been

---

31 This section is drawn from Anne Tergesen, "Universities Sued Over Plan Fees," *The Wall Street Journal* (August 10, 2016), p. C2.

targeted for offering their own mutual funds in their 401(k) plans. The Supreme Court's May, 2015 decision in *Tibble v. Edison International* put retirement plans on notice that they have a continuing duty to monitor plan investments, including fees.

Chapter 2

<><><><><><><><><><><><><><>

Today's Conventional Investment Wisdom

Chapter Overview

There is a renowned body of knowledge about financial markets called modern portfolio theory (MPT). Leading U.S. scholars completed the early development of MPT in the 1950s and 1960s. MPT has been popularized by Burton Malkiel, John Bogle and others. The purpose of MPT is to assist individual and institutional investors in making intelligent decisions, taking into account the return and risk characteristics of stocks, bonds and other asset classes. Owning a low-cost S&P 500 index fund that represents a sizeable portion of your portfolio fits perfectly with MPT.

The two early tenets of MPT—the practical implications of the academic work about financial markets—are asset allocation and the efficient market theory. Asset allocation is the investor's chosen mix of stocks and bonds in her portfolio. The efficient market theory is emphatic that investors should use the B&H strategy in conjunction with their asset allocation.

The historical record of most investors who forsake the B&H strategy has been poor—so poor that considerable fun is poked at short-term market forecasts.

The term **"modern portfolio theory" (MPT)** was coined in academia. Even if you don't recognize this imposing name, chances are good you already know something (or quite a bit) about MPT, such as reducing the stock portion of your portfolio as you approach and enter retirement (to avoid the devastating effect of a major decline in the stock market). Your knowledge comes from a financial adviser, mutual fund literature or reading (or being aware of) classic investment books by renowned authors such as (alphabetical order): Peter Bernstein, William Bernstein, John Bogle, Charles Ellis, Burton Malkiel, Paul Samuelson, William Sharpe, Jeremy Siegel, Larry Swedroe, David Swensen and Nassim Nicholas Taleb.

> "MPT has been the go-to retirement planning approach for half a century. MPT stresses the tradeoff between risk and return in investing, creating optimal portfolios based on long-term returns for a given amount of risk."[1]

A simple and helpful way to get the big picture of MPT is to use journalism's classic six questions: Who?, What?, When?, Where? Why? and How? Table 2-1 answers these questions.

Table 2-1
Six Basic Questions About Modern Portfolio Theory

1. **Who?**   Early development by a number of scholars who won the Nobel Prize in Economics

   Popularized by many leading authors including Burton Malkiel and John Bogle

2. **What?**   Choosing an appropriate asset allocation (a mix of portfolio assets) and, because of the efficient market theory, B&H that mix for the long term (with occasional adjustments)

3. **When?**   Early development during 1952–1965

4. **Where?**   Leading research universities including Chicago, Stanford and MIT

5. **Why?**   To help individual and institutional investors make intelligent decisions

6. **How?**   Implementation is based on literature and policies of mutual fund companies, counsel of financial advisers and classic investment books

The "who" answer has two parts: (1) leading scholars who won the Nobel Prize in Economics—including Harry M. Markowitz, Eugene F. Fama, William F. Sharpe and Merton H. Miller—developed two early tenets of MPT during the 1950s and 1960s and (2) various authors—especially Burton Malkiel and John Bogle—popularized MPT among investors worldwide. For example, Malkiel's best-selling book, *A Random Walk Down Wall Street,* first published in 1973, is now in its 11th edition. Early on, the "what" answer boils down to: (1) asset allocation and (2) the **efficient market theory (EMT)**, which tells investors to use the B&H strategy. Based on EMT, investors should not try to time any of the financial markets, because market timing is considered to be a fool's errand.

---

1   Mike Hogan, *Barron's* (August 22, 2016), p. 23.

As a simple summary:

Early development of MPT = Asset allocation and EMT
EMT = B&H strategy

The "when" answer indicates that MPT is about 50 years old. Certainly, the situation in the investment world was really different back then. More about that in the next chapter. The "where" answer is leading research universities. The "why" answer pertains to helping all types of investors. The "how" answer is who informs investors about MPT and assists them in the implementation process—mutual fund companies, financial advisers, and classic investment books.

Here's the bottom line: Each investor, with the help of a financial advisor, a mutual fund company or acting alone, should carefully determine his asset allocation (that is, how to divide his portfolio among the major asset classes—stocks and bonds).[2] Then, adjust that allocation in order to take less risk as he moves through the seasons of life. Whatever asset allocation is chosen, it's wise for the investor to use the B&H strategy; do not engage in market timing.

Asset Allocation

Asset allocation is deciding on and maintaining a suitable mix of stocks and bonds in your portfolio [the total of your 401(k), IRA and taxable accounts] as you age. Asset allocation is the most fundamental decision of investing.

Suppose you carefully decided on an asset mix of 60% stocks (the S&P 500) and 40% bonds. How did you make this decision? You may have filled out a questionnaire available at a mutual fund company website or consulted with a financial adviser. At its core, the decision centers on your tolerance for risk (tolerance for market fluctuations), which is heavily influenced by your age and your **longevity risk** (the unpleasant possibility of you—you and your spouse—outliving your wealth). In other words, the more you know about yourself as an investor and the history of financial markets, the more you will know what long-term asset mix is really right for your portfolio.[3]

After your asset allocation decision is implemented, you rebalance back to that allocation periodically (usually annually) and make adjustments from time to time as you age. Appendix B (pp. 83–92) discusses asset allocation in more detail; skip it if you desire.

---

2 Many experts include other asset classes, such as real estate investment trusts (REITs), precious metals and cash equivalents. To simplify, I'll limit the discussion to two major asset classes: the S&P 500 and bonds.

3 Charles D. Ellis, *Winning the Loser's Game*, 4th edition (McGraw Hill, 2002), p. 43.

Efficient Market Theory (EMT)

In an efficient financial market, market prices fully incorporate all known information. As a result, market prices change only in response to "new information." That new information is often simply called "news." Examples of such news include reports on corporate earnings and dividends, earnings forecasts, the Federal Reserve's monetary policy (especially announcements of raising or lowering interest rates), the inflation rate, consumer spending, industrial production, the price of crude oil, major legislation, U.S. Presidential and Congressional elections, and war and rumors of war. Such news tends to move the financial markets. The notion that financial markets are efficient is the basis of the EMT.

Landmark statistical studies leading to the development of the EMT found that stock prices, both individually and collectively, move in a random and unpredictable path through time—called the "random walk." The random walk resembles the aimless and unplanned lurches of a drunk trying to grab hold of a lampstand. Moreover, stock prices have no more memory than a roulette wheel or a pair of dice, and each observation is independent of the preceding observation.[4] The random walk means that each item of new information will be random in regard to being better or worse than market participants had expected.[5]

When new information comes to the stock market, no investor can afford to wait for others to act first. So they tend to act in a pack, immediately moving the price of, say, General Motors to a level that reflects this new information. But new information arrives in random fashion. Consequently, stock prices move in unpredictable ways.[6]

The EMT holds that past stock prices are a completely unreliable source for forecasting future stock prices in any way that would produce returns greater than the returns under the B&H strategy, when risk is taken into account.[7] Under the EMT, it would be impossible over the long-term for anyone to use historical data of any kind to make forecasts that would achieve higher returns and take lower risk than the S&P 500 itself. A "long-term" period virtually eliminates the element of luck in the forecasts, for the same reason that tossing a coin a large number of times is very unlikely to produce an abnormal percentage of either heads or tails. A period of, say, 30 years or more is generally regarded as the long term. Scholars have found virtually

---

4   Peter L. Bernstein, *Against the Gods* (Wiley, 1998), p. 145.

5   Larry E. Swedroe, *What Wall Street Doesn't Want You To Know* (St. Martin's Press, 2001), p. 36.

6   Peter L. Bernstein, *Against the Gods* (Wiley, 1998), p. 145.

7   Eugene F. Fama, "The Behavior of Stock Market Prices," *Journal of Business* (January 1965), p. 35.

no evidence that refutes the random walk of stock prices.[8]

Based on the EMT, it's wise for investors to use the B&H strategy. As a result, mutual fund companies urge investors to use this strategy and focus on the long-term performance of their portfolios—no matter how the financial markets move in the short term. Mutual fund companies give investors a clear message: Don't engage in market timing, and pay no attention to anyone who attempts to forecast the stock market.

The EMT regards large-cap stocks as the most efficient sector of the stock market, because there is more information available about these companies than smaller companies. As a result, profitable timing of buys and sells of the S&P 500 is thought to be impossible.

Performance of Market Timers

A practical test of the validity of the EMT is to determine whether anyone has used market timing to outperform, or "beat," the B&H strategy over the long term. To perform this test, let's examine the historical record of four main groups of market timers.

1. **Market Timing by Stock Fund Investors.** Millions of mutual fund investors engage in market timing, transferring money back and forth between stock funds and money market funds. Dalbar Inc., a financial services research firm, studied market timing by stock fund investors from 1984 through 2002. The study found those investors earned a mean annual return of 8.8% compared to the S&P 500's mean annual return of 13.5% for that period.[9] That's because investors are out of the stock market "on some really good days by trying to avoid bad ones."[10]

2. **Market Timing by Stock Fund Managers.** Most actively managed stock funds are run by managers who describe themselves as stock pickers, not market timers. Accordingly, their objective is to be fully invested in stocks, except for a "normal" percentage of fund assets—say 5%—held in cash. They maintain the cash cushion primarily to meet shareholders' redemptions that arise in the usual course of operations.

   When holding a higher-than-normal level of cash, mutual fund managers are, in effect, engaged in market timing. For example, a fund manager holding 12% cash—that is, more than double the 5% level—is forecasting a decline in the stock market. Goldman Sachs, a large Wall Street

---

8   Eugene F. Fama, "Efficient Capital Markets: A Review of Theory and Empirical Work," *Journal of Finance* (May 1970), p. 388.

9   Dalbar's periodic report, "Quantitative Analysis of Investor Behavior" (2003).

10 Spencer Jakab, "What Lousy Investors Don't Know," *The Wall Street Journal* (July 12, 2016), p. C2.

brokerage firm, studied mutual fund cash holdings from 1970 to 1989 and found that fund managers failed to call all nine major turning points in the stock market during the 1970s and 1980s.[11] Studies for other periods have reached the same conclusion. In a 1997 interview, John Bogle observed: "There is no evidence in the record of mutual fund managers showing that they have improved their performance by anticipating market changes and changing their cash positions."[12]

3. **Market Timing by Investment Strategists at the Largest Wall Street Brokerage Firms**. These strategists engage in market timing by changing the target asset allocation in their "model" (recommended) portfolios. For example, suppose a Merrill Lynch investment strategist advises an asset mix of 60% stocks and 40% bonds. Then, a few months later, she changes the allocation to 50% stock and 50% bonds. The change—selling stocks and buying bonds—is a form of market timing. It would be profitable market timing if the stock market declines and the strategist then increased the model portfolio's asset allocation to stocks. On the other hand, it would be unprofitable market timing if the stock market rises and the strategist then increased the target asset allocation to stocks.

A study spanning 1987–1996 found that market timing by investment strategists at the largest Wall Street brokerage firms beat the B&H strategy by a mere 0.18%—despite the extensive resources available to these firms. That tiny gain, almost all of which came from timing the bond market rather than the stock market, actually would have been a loss if trading costs were taken into account.[13]

4. **Market Timing by Investment Newsletters**. The leading tracker of investment newsletter performance has been *Hulbert Financial Digest*. Its study for the 20 years ending June 30, 2000, found that *The Value Line Investment Survey* had the best performance among the market timers when risk is taken into account—just slightly *below* what would have been achieved by the B&H strategy.[14]

When trading costs are taken into account, none of the four groups of market timers beat the B&H strategy. This single finding provides strong evidence that it's wise to use the B&H strategy.

Given the poor performance record of market timers, you can appreciate

---

11 Burton G. Malkiel, *A Random Walk Down Wall Street*, 5th edition (Norton, 1990), p. 179.

12 William A. Sherden, *The Fortune Sellers* (Wiley, 1998), p. 105.

13 John R. Dorfman, *The Wall Street Journal* (January 30, 1997), p. C1.

14 Robin Goldwyn Blumenthal, *Barron's* (July 17, 2000), p. 28.

this humor from Warren Buffett, a stock picker who disdains market timing. In the 1992 annual report of Berkshire Hathaway Corporation, he stated:

> "We've long felt that the only value of stock forecasters is to make fortune tellers look good. ...Short-term market forecasts are poison and should be kept locked up in a safe place, away from children and also from grown-ups who behave in the market like children."

Expert Opinions

In general, practitioners and academicians in the investment community believe that market timing—such as the grow-and-protect strategy explained in Chapters 3 and 4—is just plain foolish. Here are five expressions of that belief:

- ◆ John Bogle said: "After nearly fifty years in this business, I do not know of anybody who has done it [market timing] successfully and consistently. I don't even know anybody who *knows* anybody who has done it successfully and consistently."[15]

- ◆ Burton Malkiel said: "I have yet to see any compelling evidence that past stock prices can be used to predict future stock prices [well enough for any particular segment of the stock market to provide a higher average return while taking lower risk as compared to that segment]."[16]

- ◆ William Bernstein, a renowned financial adviser, said: "You are going to have to live with the markets the way they are—good years and bad years, occurring in a completely unpredictable sequence."[17]

- ◆ T. Rowe Price, founder of the mutual fund company that bears his name, said: "History and experience have proven that correctly predicting the timing and extent of stock market trends is impossible because world developments and the psychological reactions of people are unpredictable."[18]

- ◆ "It's quite possible that there exists some secret method of looking at [analyzing] these [historical] data which does provide superior investment results, but a large number of public efforts have uniformly resulted in failure."[19]

15 John C. Bogle, *Common Sense on Mutual Funds* (Wiley, 1999), p. 20.

16 Burton G. Malkiel, *A Random Walk Down Wall Street*, 8th edition (Norton, 2003), p. 27.

17 William J. Bernstein, *The Four Pillars of Investing* (McGraw Hill, 2002), p. 231.

18 T. Rowe Price newsletter (Fall 1987), p. 1.

19 James H. Lorie and Mary T. Hamilton, *The Stock Market: Theory and Evidence* (Irwin, 1973), p. 82.

Hulbert Financial Digest[20]

After 36 years in business, Mark Hulbert's highly influential *Hulbert Financial Digest* (*HFD*) shut down in March 2016. *HFD*, a ground-breaking newsletter, tracked the performance of investment newsletters. Prior to its launch in 1980, *HFD*'s turf was not covered; newsletters would make outrageous performance claims, and investors had little or no hope of figuring out if those brags were true.

Hulbert filled the void, buying newsletters anonymously, then following the portfolio changes recommended by the newsletter editors to see how investors would have fared. Hulbert's tracking research spoke volumes about the quality, or lack thereof, of newsletters.

"The most important lesson [of my 36 years of running the newsletter] is just how difficult it is to beat the market," Hulbert said during an appearance on "MoneyLife with Chuck Jaffe." He recalled a speech he gave when the *HFD* was in its infancy, in which he told the audience: "If we get together in 30 years [from then] and compare how [you did investmentwise for those 30 years], we'll find that almost all of you would have done better if you put all your money in the Vanguard 500 Index Fund and did nothing else for those 30 years.

"It turns out," Hulbert deadpanned, "I was being too optimistic. Hardly anyone has beaten the market over that period of time, and it's not just true of newsletters, it's true of hedge funds, it's true of mutual funds, money managers and so forth. It's even more depressing than that," he added, "because even if you took the very select group that has beaten the market and looked at them alone going forward, you would find most of them fail to beat the market [in the future]."

Hulbert maintains most of the short-term gains posted by a manager or a strategy can be attributed to luck. And even if you find someone who beats the market, their edge is likely to be so narrow that it's hardly worth the effort.

I conclude this section with a long excerpt from an informative article by Mark Hulbert in 2013:[21]

> "If you think you will know it when the bull market [which started March 9, 2009] finally comes to an end, you're kidding yourself.
>
> The vast majority of professional advisers who try to get in and out of the stock market at the right time end up doing worse than those who simply buy and hold through bull and bear markets alike. Even

---

20 Much of the material in the first part of this section is from Chuck Jaffe's MarketWatch column (March 11, 2016).

21 Mark Hulbert, "Can Market Timers Beat the [S&P 500] Index?," *The Wall Street Journal* (July 20–21, 2013), p. B7.

those few who beat a buy-and-hold strategy during one period rarely beat it in the next one.

What makes you so confident you can do better?

A surer strategy is to keep a steady [asset mix] through thick and thin. If you are frightened by the prospect of another bear market, then you should reduce your equity [stock] holdings now to whatever level you would be comfortable holding through one.

Though that means you will miss out on gains if the market keeps rising, odds are that you will more than make up for it by losing less in the next bear market.

Consider the investment adviser—among the more than 200 tracked by *Hulbert Financial Digest*—who did the best job of sidestepping the 2000–02 bear market, during which the S&P 500 fell 49%, and getting back into stocks close to the beginning of the subsequent bull market.

He is Bob Brinker, editor of an advisory service called *Bob Brinker's Marketimer*. Mr. Brinker told clients to sell most of their equity holdings in January 2000 [January 10, 2000], just four days before the Dow hit its bull market high. His recommendation to get back into stocks came within less than 4% of the October 2002 bear market low.

The situations in both early 2000 and early 2003 were "textbook" examples of major market turning points, he says.

Unfortunately, his success didn't carry over to the next market cycle. Mr. Brinker says he failed to anticipate the 2007–09 bear market because it was historically unique—'a once-in-a lifetime financial train wreck.'

As a result, he kept his model portfolios 100% in equities throughout the bear market decline, which was even more severe than the one following the popping of the Internet bubble [2000–2002]. His portfolios on average shed about half their value [in 2007–2009].

Mr. Brinker's failure is typical."

Poking Fun at Short-Term Forecasts

Virtually no one believes it is possible to use past prices (or any other historical data) to make short-term forecasts of the stock market that, over the long term, achieve higher returns and take lower risk than the B&H

strategy. The general lack of success in making accurate short-term forecasts of the stock market over the years has led knowledgeable investors to use this analogy: Forecasting the stock market based on past prices is like trying to drive a car by looking in the rearview mirror.

Because the vast majority of investors believe—and may have found out first-hand—that accurate short-term forecasting of the stock market appears to be impossible, this story is told about Albert Einstein. When he died, Albert was warmly greeted by St. Peter at heaven's gate. In the conversation, St. Peter asked: "Would you be willing to stay in a dorm with three roommates until your plush cottage is ready next week?" Albert graciously agreed. St. Peter told Albert that one of his roommates has an IQ of 160, another's IQ is 120, but apologized for the third roommate's IQ being 100." Albert replied, "That's all right. I'll discuss higher mathematics with the first one. With the second, I'll talk about the upcoming NFL draft. I'll ask the third what he thinks the S&P 500 will do next year!"

Summary and Conclusions for Part One

The S&P 500, the U.S.'s premier stock index, is a widely-accepted benchmark of the stock market. The 500 companies in the S&P 500—all headquartered in the U.S.—represent about 80% of the total market value of all publicly traded U.S. stocks and some 40% of the total market value of all publicly traded stocks in the entire world. As a group, the 500 companies have a massive global reach: They derive about one-third of their sales abroad. Over the past 20 years, the S&P 500 outperformed all other major world stock indexes when risk is taken into account.

For 1966–2015, the S&P 500 had a mean annual return of 11%. Along with this return came considerable risk in the form of 15 declines ranging from –19% to –57%.

A major tenet underlying modern portfolio theory—today's conventional investment wisdom—is that financial markets are efficient. This means the markets fully incorporate all available information in setting their prices. As a result, those prices are unpredictable in the short term. If the stock market is, in fact, efficient, it would be impossible for anyone to make forecasts of the S&P 500 that, over the long term, would achieve a higher return and take lower risk compared to buying-and-holding (B&H) the S&P 500. That's why the B&H strategy is considered to be the wise choice for investors, and market timing the S&P 500—an investor moving out of the index in anticipation of a decline and moving into the index in anticipation of an advance—is thought to be a fool's errand.

At this point in the book, are you persuaded to use the low-cost B&H strategy? The evidence presented so far makes a strong case for this strategy. Despite the S&P 500's occasional volatility, the mean annual return for almost all 20-year periods has been at or near 11%. If you (you and your financial adviser) can control your emotions during periods of volatility, the B&H strategy—for a portion of or all of your stock portfolio—seems like a slam dunk.

Andrew Bary recently made this confirming statement in *Barrons:*[22]

> "A buy-and-hold investor in a Standard & Poor's 500 index fund has been able to top nearly all endowments in the past year and the past five years ended June 30—when endowment fiscal years end—and beaten most over 10 years. Simpler [endowments use very complex asset allocations] has been better."

But can there be a better strategy than B&H? We will explore this question in Chapters 3–5.

I welcome your comments and questions on Chapters 1 and 2 at harrisjohnk@hotmail.com

---

22 Andrew Bary, "A Hard Lesson for Endowments," *Barron's* (November 20, 2017), p. 11.

PART TWO

Investing in the S&P 500:
The Grow-and-Protect (G&P) Strategy

Chapters 3 and 4 present the back-tested results for 1966–2015 for growing-and-protecting wealth: the G&P strategy. The G&P strategy involves market timing using a low-cost S&P 500 exchange-traded fund. Therefore, the G&P strategy flies in the face of today's conventional investment wisdom. Facts about the G&P strategy's returns and risk will be illuminating to all types of investors. I'm optimistic that the G&P strategy will beat the B&H strategy as the future unfolds.

Chapter 5 sets the stage for the live test of the G&P strategy versus the B&H strategy. The test officially began on October 14, 2016, the day this book was published. This test should be exciting, and its results over many years could overturn some of today's conventional investment wisdom. Time will tell.

Chapter 3

◇◇◇◇◇◇◇◇◇◇◇◇◇◇◇

The G&P Strategy's Returns

Chapter Overview

It is possible the efficient market theory (EMT), a tenet of modern portfolio theory, could be invalid now. Regardless of whether EMT is valid or invalid, investors would benefit from having some form of wealth insurance—for a price—as protection in case of a disaster in the stock market, just as they have homeowner's insurance to protect their house and its contents from a sizable loss. The grow-and-protect (G&P) strategy introduced in this chapter would have been a very effective form of wealth self-insurance during 1966–2015.

The annual returns for the G&P strategy compared to the B&H strategy strongly favor the G&P strategy. Back-testing for 1966–2015 indicates the G&P strategy's superior returns were largest during the 15 bear markets during that period.

From October 9, 2007 (a bull market top) to March 9, 2009 (a bear market bottom), the S&P 500 lost a whopping 57%—one of the most severe bear markets in history. I was fortunate because I sold my TIAA Real Estate Fund (the only stock-type investment I owned at the time) and went to cash on August 4, 2008. As a result I did not suffer most of the decline.

On the other hand, my research partner, Kip Karney, was not so fortunate. To put it bluntly, Kip—like millions of other investors—took a big hit in his 401(k) portfolio.

Kip and I had lunch (fried chicken, as usual) in the Spring of 2010. By then the S&P 500 had had a strong rally off the March 2009 bear-market low. Obviously, Kip was feeling much better about his portfolio. At some point during lunch, he said something that caught me off guard: "I'd like to buy some wealth insurance to protect my portfolio in the next bear market."

I'd never heard of wealth insurance, so I asked him about it. He said he had homeowner's insurance for his house and its contents in case of a sizable loss. Why not have insurance to cover the possibility of another major decline in his wealth? I quipped: "Why don't you just call Prudential or State Farm and buy a wealth-insurance policy?" We laughed, but for the next several weeks we discussed the topic.

Eventually, we linked the concept of wealth insurance to the activity of market timing. A S&P 500 market timer tries to be invested in most of the Index's good (up) times but to not be invested in some of its bad (down) times. Since we could engage in market timing ourselves using a low-cost S&P 500 ETF—with or without success—the concept of wealth insurance morphed into the concept of **wealth self-insurance**.[1] This was an important breakthrough in our stock market research. This chapter and the next discuss the result of that work—the grow-and-protect (G&P) strategy.[2]

Changes Facilitating Market Timing

Since the early development of MPT was completed in the 1960s, four major changes have occurred. All of them facilitate market timing.

1. **Trading costs.** The 1960s trading costs were approximately 2% of the total market value of a trade to either buy or sell. Today most trades are under $10 to buy or sell, regardless of the total market value of the trade. Low trading costs facilitate short-term trading.

2. **Revolution in computer technology.** In the mid 1960s, the computer industry was in its early stages. The only option was to do computer work on a mainframe computer. The personal computer industry emerged in the 1980s. Software, such as Microsoft's Excel, became available then to prepare electronic spreadsheets. Electronic spreadsheets can be used to search for historical stock market patterns that repeat themselves with enough consistency to be profitably exploited—if such patterns exist and can be found. This data-mining research is based on formulas, data sorting and data coloring. In fact, this is how the G&P strategy (Chapters 3–4) was developed.

3. **Exchange-traded funds (ETFs).** These funds, which often mimic an index (for example, the S&P 500), were introduced in the 1990s. As you saw in Table 1-3 (p. 16), some S&P 500 ETFs have a low cost. That's because there is no high-dollar professional money manager involved. Basically, a correctly programmed computer can "manage" an S&P 500 ETF with very

---

1   Later in this chapter, wealth self-insurance is quantified for the G&P strategy.

2   If you have not read Appendix G (pp. 131–143), now is an appropriate time to do so.

little human involvement needed. S&P 500 ETFs trade throughout the day like individual stocks.

4. **Data availability and statistical learning.** A new frontier has emerged: The interplay of new and readily accessible sources of data and cutting-edge advances in the field of statistical learning. I believe my S&P 500 database for 1966–2015 is virtually 100% accurate (that is, as good as anyone else's S&P 500 database for this period).

Considered collectively, I think these four developments raise a reasonable possibility that the EMT could be proven to be invalid. In that regard, this chapter and the next provide background for the live test described in Chapter 5.

Appendix C (p. 93) presents a brief discussion of behavioral finance, a field of study that raises questions about the validity of the EMT.

A Sample of the G&P Strategy's Performance[3]

The watchword of the G&P strategy is: "Sell, then buy lower." Specifically, that means selling a low-cost S&P 500 ETF and trying to buy it back later at a lower price. Historically, a buy or sell trade has occurred, on average, about once every 2½ months—certainly not an onerous amount of trading.

Keep in mind the G&P strategy and the B&H strategy perform exactly the same when the traffic signal is green. *The time the signal is red accounts for all of the difference in performance between the two strategies.*

An investor using the G&P strategy could be out of the S&P 500 on some of its best days. But the opposite situation could occur, not being invested in the S&P 500 on some of its worst days.

It has been said that the stock market (S&P 500) "takes the stairs up and the elevator down."[4] The recommendation for the G&P strategy is: Don't spend much time on the elevator!

The day I wrote this section (August 11, 2016), the S&P 500 closed at a new all-time high.[5] This bull market started March 9, 2009. To date, it's the second longest bull market in history, nearly 7½ years and counting; the total gain is 223%.

What will cause the current bull market to end? A speculative bubble bursting? The U.S. economy going into a recession? Worldwide negative interest rates? A war or rumor of war? And when will this bull market end? Under the G&P strategy

---

3   As you read the remaining sections of this chapter, keep in mind the G&P strategy was developed by data mining, just as the B&H strategy was developed by data mining (p. 13).

4   A Seeking Alpha Internet article by Andrew Hecht (September 15, 2015).

5   The Dow and the NASDAQ Composite also hit new all-time highs on August 11, 2016. This was the first triple-record day since December 31, 1999.

discussed in this chapter and the next, history will be our guide.

What I do know is the date when the traffic signal turned from green to red correctly predicting the end of each of the 15 bull markets since 1966. Table 3-1 presents the relevant data. On average, the first sell signal occurred 1.8 months after the bull market top. The shortest time to the first sell signal after the top was 0.1 months in 1973, and the longest was 6.2 months in 1976–1977.

Table 3-1
First Sell Signal After the Seven Bull Market Tops, 1966–2015

Bull Market Top		First Sell Signal After Top		Time Between Top and First Sell Signal	Change in S&P 500 During that Period	Bear Market	
Date (1)	S&P 500 (2)	Date (3)	S&P 500 (4)	(months) (5)	(6)	Months (7)	Change (8)
02/09/66	94.06	02/23/66	91.48	0.5	−2.7%	7.9	−22.1%
11/29/68	108.37	02/24/69	98.60	2.8	−9.0%	17.9	−36.1%
01/11/73	120.24	01/16/73	118.14	0.1	−1.7%	20.7	−48.2%
09/21/76	107.83	03/22/77	101.00	6.2	−6.3%	17.5	−19.4%
11/28/80	140.52	12/10/80	128.26	0.4	−8.7%	20.5	−27.1%
08/25/87	336.77	10/14/87	305.23*	1.7	−9.4%	3.3	−33.5%
07/16/90	368.95	08/03/90	344.86	0.6	−6.5%	2.9	−19.9%
07/17/98	1186.75	07/24/98	1140.80	0.2	−3.0%	1.4	−19.3%
03/24/00	1527.46	09/22/00	1448.72	5.9	−5.2%	12.3	−27.8%
05/21/01	1312.83	None		Not applicable		4.0	−26.4%
01/04/02	1172.51	None		Not applicable		6.7	−32.0%
08/22/02	962.70	09/18/02	869.46	0.9	−9.7%	1.6	−19.3%
10/09/07	1565.15	10/19/07	1500.63	0.3	−4.1%	13.4	−51.9%
01/06/09	924.70	01/22/09	827.50	0.4	−4.5%	2.1	−27.6%
04/29/11	1363.61	07/27/11	1304.89	3.1	−4.3%	5.1	−19.4%
Mean				1.8	−5.8%	8.8	−28.7%

*The largest Crash in the S&P 500's history occurred October 19, 1987; the decline that day was 20.5%.

Note that using my criterion for a bear market of −19% rather than Wall Street's criterion of −20% identifies five additional bear markets.

The mean decline from the bull market top to the first sell signal was 5.8%. The range was 1.7% in 1973 to 9.7% in 2002. It is noteworthy that the first sell signal after the bull market top in 1987 occurred only three trading days before the Crash on October 19, 1987.

If you want to pick the exact top day of the current bull market, you would not want to go by the G&P strategy. It never predicted the very top day, but it came rather close a few times.

Before we examine the annual returns of the G&P strategy compared to the B&H strategy, let's consider some more history. Two noteworthy events in the past 20 years were: (1) Alan Greenspan using the phrase "irrational exuberance" in December 1996 and (2) Britain voting June 23, 2016 to leave the European Economic Community (Brexit).

Alan Greenspan, then Chairman of the Federal Reserve, coined the term "irrational exuberance" in a televised speech at the American Enterprise Institute on the evening of December 5, 1996. Here's the actual question he raised:

> "But how do we know when irrational exuberance has unduly escalated asset values, which then become subject to unexpected and prolonged contractions as they have in Japan over the last decade?"

How did the S&P 500 react to Greenspan's question? It actually closed higher two days later, but then fell 3.8% in five days, before rising 26% in the next 16 months. The traffic signal was green that whole time.

The outcome of Britain voting to exit the European Economic Community came as a total shock. On the day of the voting, British bookmakers set the odds at only 1:7 that the exit would occur. Do you know how the S&P 500 reacted in this case? After falling 5.3% in the two trading days after the vote, the S&P 500 rose 9.3% to a new all-time record high on August 11, 2016 (the day I wrote this section). This rally, like the one after Greenspan's speech, made it feel as if somewhere a power switch had been flipped on.[6] The traffic signal has been green since February 24, 2016. From that buy signal to August 11, 2016, the S&P 500 gained 13.3%. For 2016, as of August 11th, the G&P strategy had gained 11.7% versus 6.9% for the B&H strategy. Of course, all these figures come from back-testing the G&P strategy. *The proof of the pudding is in how a market-timing strategy performs in real time.* The day this book was published (October 14, 2016) launched the live test of the strategy, discussed in Chapter 5.

G&P Strategy Returns, 1966–2015

Table 3-2 presents the G&P **strategy's annual return** compared to the B&H return for the S&P 500 for each year during 1966–2015.

---

6   Vito J. Racanelli, The Trader column, *Barron's* (July 18, 2016), p. M3.

Table 3-2
G&P Returns vs. B&H Returns for the S&P 500, 1966–2015

The "Difference in Return" in each bear-market year is shaded to identify it. For analytical purposes, I define a bear market as an S&P 500 decline of at least 19% (rather than the conventional definition of a 20% decline).

To be user-friendly, all the figures have been rounded to the nearest full percentage point. For example for 1968, 12% − 11% = 0% is due to rounding.

Year (1)	Number of Trades (2)	G&P Return (3)	B&H Return (S&P 500) (4)	Difference in Return: G&P − B&H (5)	Wealth Self-Insurance Paid (n = 14) (6)
1966	12	4%	−10%	17%	
1967	2	26%	24%	2%	
1968	2	12%	11%	0%	
1969	10	−1%	−9%	7%	
1970	6	34%	4%	31%	
1971	6	13%	14%	−1%	1%
1972	6	14%	19%	−5%	5%
1973	12	3%	−15%	18%	
1974	14	−5%	−26%	21%	
1975	0	37%	37%	0%	
1976	0	24%	24%	0%	
1977	4	−1%	−7%	5%	
1978	3	10%	7%	3%	
1979	5	17%	18%	−1%	1%
1980	4	41%	32%	9%	
1981	2	−3%	−5%	2%	
1982	6	30%	21%	8%	
1983	0	23%	23%	0%	
1984	4	7%	6%	1%	
1985	2	28%	32%	−4%	4%
1986	0	18%	18%	0%	
1987	6	26%	5%	21%	
1988	0	17%	17%	0%	
1989	2	28%	31%	−3%	3%
1990	10	3%	−3%	6%	
1991	2	28%	31%	−3%	3%
1992	2	2%	8%	−6%	6%
1993	0	10%	10%	0%	
1994	8	−1%	1%	−2%	2%
1995	0	37%	37%	0%	
1996	2	21%	23%	−2%	2%

Table 3-2 (continued)

Year (1)	Number of Trades (2)	G&P Return (3)	B&H Return (S&P 500) (4)	Difference in Return: G&P – B&H (5)	Wealth Self-Insurance Paid (n = 14) (6)
1997	0	33%	33%	0%	
1998	10	34%	29%	5%	
1999	6	20%	21%	−1%	1%
2000	5	−4%	−9%	5%	
2001	3	6%	−12%	18%	
2002	4	2%	−22%	24%	
2003	2	31%	29%	2%	
2004	2	12%	11%	1%	
2005	4	3%	5%	−2%	2%
2006	2	12%	16%	−3%	3%
2007	7	6%	5%	0%	
2008	13	4%	−37%	41%	
2009	2	52%	26%	26%	
2010	4	12%	15%	−3%	3%
2011	6	8%	2%	6%	
2012	6	6%	16%	−9%	9%
2013	6	31%	32%	−2%	2%
2014	3	15%	14%	1%	
2015	10	5%	1%	3%	
Total	227				
Mean	4.5	16%	11%	6%	3%

Here are six astounding observations regarding the data in Table 3-2:

1. The bottom line indicates the G&P strategy's mean annual return (1966–2015) was 16% versus 11% for the B&H strategy. The difference of 6% does not add across because of rounding to the nearest full percentage point. Using two decimals, the bottom line would be:

	G&P Return	B&H Return (S&P 500)	Difference in Return: G&P – B&H
Mean	15.87%	11.12%	5.75%

The G&P strategy generated this very impressive performance by making 227 trades during 1966–2015, a mean of 4.5 trades per year.

2. The G&P strategy's best outperformance compared to the B&H strategy consistently occurred during bear markets:

Bear Market Year	Difference in return: G&P – B&H
2008	37%
1970	31%
2009	27%
2002	24%
1974	21%
1987	21%
1973	18%
2001	18%

The worse the year's return for the B&H strategy, the better the year's return for the G&P strategy.

3. Chapter 1 pointed out that a $1,000 investment made at the beginning of 1966 under the B&H strategy would have grown to $101,361 at the end of 2015. The wondrous total accumulation of a $1,000 investment at the beginning of 1966 under the G&P strategy would be $975,836, or 9.6 times as much as the B&H strategy. Yes, you read these figures correctly.

4. A $1,000 investment made at the beginning of each of the five 10-year periods in Table 3-2 resulted in these total accumulations at the end of those periods:

	G&P Strategy	B&H Strategy	Increased Return Under G&P
1966–1975	$3,327	$1,380	$1,947
1976–1985	$4,673	$3,816	$857
1986–1995	$4,498	$3,991	$507
1996–2005	$3,669	$2,386	$1,293
2006–2015	$3,803	$2,022	$1,781

5. The period 2000–2009 has been referred to as "The lost decade for stock investors." The reason: The B&H strategy had a negative return for the decade. That is, a $1,000 investment in the S&P 500 at the beginning of 2000 had a total value of $909 at the end of 2009. In contrast, a $1,000 investment at the beginning of 2000 under the G&P strategy would have accumulated $2,955 at the end of 2009—a 225% improvement over B&H.

6. Column (6) indicates wealth self-insurance was paid when column (5) was negative—that is, **G&P** underperformed **B&H**. That happened in 14 of the 50 years (28% of the time). *All 14 of these years occurred during bull markets,* times when the **G&P** investor could have most easily afforded to pay for the wealth self-insurance.

7. *Appendix H (pp. 143–146) provides a big takeaway from analyzing Table 3-2.*

I believe these seven observations about the data in Table 3-2 are aptly described in Proverbs 27:12a (New International Version, NIV):

The prudent see danger and take refuge.

The next chapter examines the **G&P** strategy's risk in comparison to the risk of the **B&H** strategy. So as not to keep you in suspense, **G&P**'s risk is much lower than **B&H**'s risk.

Chapter 4

◇◇◇◇◇◇◇◇◇◇◇◇◇◇

The G&P Strategy's Risk

Chapter Overview

Two measures of risk— (1) negative annual returns and (2) the minimum number of calendar years needed to recoup the maximum loss—are used in this chapter to measure the G&P strategy's risk compared to the B&H strategy's risk. A look at the G&P strategy's *sell-to-buy trades* also sheds light on the market-timing risk.

As we saw in Chapter 1, the risk of owning the S&P 500 is the uncertainty of its future market value. The chapter spotlights the G&P **strategy's risk**. One measure of that risk is to compare the negative annual returns under the G&P and B&H strategies:

G&P Strategy		B&H Strategy	
Number	Range	Number	Range
6	−1% to −5%	11	−3% to −37%

Under the G&P strategy, the last year having a negative return was 2000 (−4%). In contrast for 2000–2015, the B&H strategy had negative returns four times: −9% (2000), −12% (2001), −22% (2002) and −37% (2008). These statistics indicate much lower risk for the G&P strategy.

Rolling Mean Annual Returns

We saw in Chapter 1 (p. 11) that a 7-calendar-year mean annual return was required to essentially assure that the B&H strategy would not have had a loss while holding the S&P 500. Table 4-1, column (2), reveals that a 2-calendar-year mean annual return is the comparable statistic for the G&P strategy. This finding is awesome!

Table 4-1
G&P Strategy's 2-Calendar-Year Mean Annual Returns, Trades and Trading Days Spent Out of the S&P 500, 1966–2015

Year (1)	2-Calendar-Year Mean Annual Return (2)	Number of Trades (3)	Trading Days Spent Out of S&P 500 (4)
1966		12	85
1967	16.3%	2	24
1968	18.8%	2	11
1969	5.0%	10	102
1970	16.6%	6	79
1971	24.7%	6	40
1972	14.1%	6	93
1973	8.5%	12	100
1974	−1.0%	14	93
1975	15.9%	0	0
1976	30.5%	0	0
1977	11.0%	4	79
1978	4.1%	3	43
1979	13.7%	5	37
1980	29.4%	4	37
1981	19.2%	2	13
1982	13.3%	6	72
1983	26.1%	0	0
1984	14.7%	4	59
1985	17.6%	2	22
1986	23.4%	0	0
1987	28.3%	6	25
1988	27.4%	0	0
1989	22.6%	2	50
1990	15.7%	10	55
1991	15.3%	2	22
1992	14.7%	2	38
1993	5.8%	0	0
1994	4.6%	8	65
1995	18.3%	0	0
1996	29.1%	2	11
1997	27.1%	0	0
1998	33.5%	10	56

Table 4-1 (continued)
G&P Strategy's 2-Calendar-Year Mean Annual Returns, Trades and Trading Days Spent Out of the S&P 500, 1966–2015

Year (1)	2-Calendar-Year Mean Annual Return (2)	Number of Trades (3)	Trading Days Spent Out of S&P 500 (4)
1999	26.6%	6	55
2000	7.9%	5	59
2001	1.2%	3	153
2002	4.0%	4	103
2003	14.0%	2	32
2004	19.2%	2	29
2005	8.9%	4	36
2006	9.1%	2	11
2007	9.2%	7	72
2008	5.1%	13	71
2009	29.0%	2	28
2010	32.8%	4	58
2011	9.8%	6	27
2012	7.5%	6	30
2013	19.0%	6	43
2014	23.9%	3	33
2015	10.9%	10	75
Total		227	2,226
Mean		4.5	45

Additional Characteristics of G&P's Risk Profile

Now, consider the other two columns in Table 4-1. They are important for two reasons. First, consider the bottom two rows:

	Number of Trades	Trading Days Spent Out of S&P 500
Total	227	2,226
Mean per year	4.5	45

The mean number of trades was 4.5 per year. Scanning column (3), you will see there were eight years when no trades occurred: 1975, 1976, 1983, 1986, 1988,

1993, 1995 and 1997. Based on their returns in Table 3-2, the mean annual return for these eight years was 25%—more than double the 1966–2015 mean annual return of 11%.

Second, the 2,226 trading days spent out of the S&P 500 was 18% of all the trading days during 1966–2015. *These "red traffic signal days" accounted for all of the difference in performance between the G&P strategy and the B&H strategy.* The G&P investor's wealth would have held steady for those 2,226 trading days, thereby reducing risk—a safety-first approach.[1] In Table 3-2 we saw the G&P's mean annual return for the 50 years exceeded B&H's mean annual return by an impressive 6%. The S&P 500 tended to be in a declining mode for the trading days spent out of the Index.

Let's take a close look at the outcomes of the 113 *sell-to-buy* trades (times when the traffic signal was red)—that is, specifically what happened during those times:

- ◆ 70 of these trades (62%) were winners (gainers); the mean gain was 5.3%; the largest gain was 26.3% in 1987 (being out of the S&P 500 at the time of the Crash on October 19, 1987); and 11 of the gainers were double digits.

- ◆ The other 43 of these trades (38%) were losers; the mean loss was 3.0%; the largest loss was 7.1%; and 11 of the losers were 5% or more.

Having an occasional losing market-timing trade need not be disastrous. To that point, Ken Fisher, a long-time *Forbes* columnist and renowned money manager, observed:[2]

> "Getting defensive successfully, even if you don't do it perfectly, can provide you a major and lasting performance boost."

So, that's a description of the G&P strategy's risk profile. All things considered, this strategy had much lower risk than the B&H strategy.

---

1   Have you ever heard Dick Vitale do the commentary for a basketball game on TV? If so, you know when he analyzes plays, he stops the replay by saying: "Freeze it." Similarly, the 2,317 trading days freeze the G&P investor's wealth.

2   Kenneth L. Fisher, *The Only Three Questions That Count: Investing by Knowing What Others Don't* (Wiley 2007) p. 277.

Chapter 5

◇◇◇◇◇◇◇◇◇◇◇◇◇◇◇◇

Let the Live Test Begin!

Chapter Overview

The brand new **G&P** strategy carries a warning label: Its past results are all from back testing for the 1966–2015 period. The live test of the strategy began November 2017, the date this Revised First Edition was published. The strategy's trading rules are proprietary; if the rules were divulged, the future performance of the strategy might be jeopardized.

In the live test, will the **G&P** strategy outperform the **B&H** strategy? History can be a guide to shape investors' expectations about the strategy's performance in the future.

Watching the **G&P** strategy perform in real time going forward can be like viewing a sporting event. This spectator activity is accomplished by regularly visiting the free companion website for the book (gandpresearch.com).

Three relevant topics are discussed late in the chapter: (1) why the current bull market will end, (2) high stock valuations and (3) the presence of worldwide ultra-low and even negative interest rates.

Along with many other people, I think there is a lot of street-smart, hard-knocks wisdom in country music songs. The songwriters may be telling about their own life experiences or the life experiences of others. An example is "Warning Labels" sung by Doug Stone. Here are the opening lyrics:

> I begged her to stay. I said give me one more try.
> But she said it's over. Then she said goodbye.
> Now I'm at this bar trying to wash away the pain.
> But every time I hear the jukebox, the tears fall like rain.
> They ought to put warning labels on those sad country songs.

Like sad country songs, there ought to be a warning label on every market-timing strategy. In the case of the G&P strategy, part of the warning label relates to the fact that 100% of its results are from back-testing for 1966–2015. Of course for the G&P strategy, the proof will be in the pudding: How it performs in live testing, which began November 2017. The other part of the warning label is that no other back-tested, market-timing strategy in the history of Wall Street has had results even half as good as the results of the G&P strategy.

Regardless of how great the back-tested performance is, market-timing strategies tend to fail during live testing. For example, I report in Chapter 7 that five of the market-timing strategies I tracked or developed and tracked failed. The TIAA Real Estate Fund strategy was the only success. The last one on my list is the G&P strategy. Time will tell if it succeeds or fails.

The G&P strategy's live test is a classic David versus Goliath confrontation. Of course, David is the G&P strategy, and Goliath is the B&H strategy. In the biblical account of David versus Goliath, I believe that God knew beforehand that David, the young Jewish shepherd boy, would use a sling—invoking God's name—and kill Goliath, the nine-foot Philistine giant. Similarly, God knows the outcome of the G&P strategy—but it's unknown to anyone else.

Keeping a Secret

A **financial market anomaly** is any investment strategy that, over a long period, generated abnormal returns—returns which, after taking risk into account, exceeded the market's mean return for that long period. Many leading scholars believe that the abnormal returns of any market anomaly discovered and divulged to the public—for example, by publishing a book or an article describing it—will likely be eliminated as a result of the competition among investors trying to capitalize on the anomaly.[1]

Although that argument appears to be sound, history does not always bear it out. Let's consider the "January Effect" market anomaly: The increase in the prices of small-cap stocks for January is far greater than for any other month. This calendar effect would create an opportunity for investors to buy small-cap stocks for lower prices before January and sell them after their prices increase. By my count during 1983–1985, 10 articles on the January Effect appeared in top-tier academic journals. In 1996, a well-researched article reported the January Effect had not been eliminated.[2]

Even though the January Effect lives on, I've decided not to divulge the

---

1   William F. Sharpe, Gordon J. Alexander and Jeffery V. Bailey, *Investments*, 6th edition (Prentice Hall, 1999), p. 96.

2   Robert A. Haugen and Philippe Jorion, "The January Effect: Still There After All these Years," *Financial Analysts Journal* (January–February, 1996), pp. 27–31.

mathematical formulas that are the basis of the G&P strategy. Why should I take a chance that the G&P market anomaly could be eliminated if it were divulged?

> "A moment's thought will show that there can be no such thing as a scientific prediction of economic events under human control. The very 'dependability' of such a prediction will cause human actions which will invalidate it. Hence thoughtful chartists admit that continued success is dependent upon keeping the successful method known to only a few people."[3]

The G&P strategy is based on **technical analysis**. Technical analysis uses data generated by the stock market itself or data from any other source to forecast the stock market (in this book, forecast the direction the S&P 500). Appendix D (pp. 95–110) is a note to those interested in technical analysis.

Who Can Use the G&P Strategy?

◆ Individual investors having an employer-sponsored retirement plan [401(k), 403(b), 457 or Thrift Savings Plan], a Traditional IRA, a SEP IRA or a Roth IRA.

◆ Individual investors having taxable accounts. (Of course, trades in these accounts are subject to income taxes that diminish returns, depending on the investor's particular circumstances.)

◆ Institutional investors: pension funds, endowments and foundations.

Who Should Use the G&P Strategy?

We learned this history lesson in Chapters 3–4: Compared to the B&H strategy, the G&P strategy achieved much higher returns and took much lower risk for 1966–October 14, 2016. Nonetheless, nobody should seriously consider using the G&P strategy unless it establishes a desirable track record in the live test.

Suppose the G&P strategy does establish a desirable track record over the next (say) three years, and you decide to use the strategy for some portion of your asset allocation to stocks. In that case, keep this valuable insight in mind:[4]

> "As difficult as it is to sell when stock prices are high and everyone is optimistic, it is more difficult to buy at market bottoms when

---

3   Benjamin Graham and David Dodd, Security analysis, 2nd edition (McGraw Hill, 1940), pp. 715–716. Cited in Jeremy J. Siegel, *Stocks for the Long Run*, 4th edition (McGraw Hill, 2008), p. 304.

4   Jeremy J. Siegel, *Stocks for the Long Run*, 4th edition (McGraw Hill, 2008), p. 27..

pessimism is widespread and few have the confidence to venture back into stocks."

As with the B&H strategy, investors using the G&P strategy must control their emotions.

Here is a repeat of John Bogle's sage advice for choosing an appropriate investment strategy:[5]

> "Although there is no guarantee that...patterns of the past, no matter how deeply ingrained in the historical record, will prevail in the future, a study of the past, accompanied by a self-administered dose of common sense, is the intelligent investor's best course."

Shaping Future Expectations

As Table 4–1 (pp. 46–47) indicates, there were 227 trades during 1966–2015. That's a mean of 4.5 trades per year. Eight of the 50 years had no trades.

Under the G&P strategy, there are two types of trades: (1) sell-to-buy trades that occur during red-signal periods—which are what account for the difference in performance between G&P and B&H—and (2) buy-to-sell trades that occur during green-signal periods. For the 113 sell-to-buy trades during the back-tested period, the mean outcome was a gain of 2.0% in 20 trading days. For the 114 buy-to-sell trades, the mean outcome was a gain of 5.7% in 90 trading days. *Note that on some occasions, the trades are only a few days apart.*

On the day this book was originally published (October 14, 2016), the G&P strategy was on a buy signal, which occurred February 24, 2016 (S&P 500 1929.80). When the next sell signal occurs, history tells us what to expect:

Outcome of Sell-to-Buy Trades	Portion of Trades	Mean Outcome	Remarks
2.00% or more gain	43.6%	7.0%	Best trade 26.3%
0.00% to 1.99%	17.1%	1.2%	
−0.01% to −1.99%	12.8%	−1.2%	
−2.00% or more loss	26.5%	−3.8%	Worst trade −7.1%
	100.0%		

Then, when the next buy signal occurs, history again tells us what to expect:

---

5   John C. Bogle, *Common Sense on Mutual Funds* (Wiley, 1999), p. 6.

Outcome of Buy-to-Sell Trades	Portion of Trades	Mean Outcome	Remarks
2.00% or more gain	42.7%	16.1%	Best trade 65.1%
0.00% to 1.99%	20.5%	0.9%	
−0.01% to −1.99%	14.5%	−1.1%	
−2.00% or more loss	22.3%	−4.6%	Worst trade −7.5%
	100.0%		

Let's consider two other historical sources of information to shape our future expectations. First, each bull market top since 1966, the first sell signal after the top, the S&P 500 decline and the number of sell signals that followed during the bear market:

Bull Market Top	First Sell Signal After the Top	S&P 500 Decline	Number of Sell Signals During the Bear Market
02/09/66	02/23/66	2.7%	6
11/29/68	02/24/69	9.0%	7
01/13/73	01/16/73	1.7%	12
09/21/76	03/27/77	6.3%	3
11/28/80	12/10/80	8.7%	5
08/25/87	10/14/87	9.4%	3
07/16/90	08/03/90	6.5%	3
07/17/98	07/24/98	3.0%	2
03/24/00	09/22/00	5.2%	3
08/22/02	09/18/02	9.7%	1
10/09/07	10/19/07	4.1%	8
01/06/09	01/22/09	4.5%	1
04/29/11	07/27/11	4.3%	3
Mean		5.8%	4

Second, the S&P 500 can turn on a dime, either up or down. This phenomenon is prevalent during bear markets. Three cases illustrate:

Case	Dates	Trading Days	S&P 500 Change
1	10/13/87 to 10/19/87	4	−28.5%
	10/19/87 to 10/21/87	2	14.9%
2	07/05/02 to 07/23/02	12	−19.3%
	07/23/02 to 07/31/02	6	14.3%
3	09/30/08 to 10/10/08	8	−22.9%
	10/10/08 to 10/13/08	1	11.6%

The huge "selling climaxes" on 10/19/87, 07/23/02 and 10/10/08 were opportunities to buy the S&P 500 at fire-sale prices.

Watching the G&P Strategy Perform

Watching the G&P's performance is somewhat like watching a sporting event. During the time the traffic signal is green, the G&P investor roots for the S&P 500 to rise. And he roots for the S&P 500 to fall during the time the signal is red. Although using the G&P strategy would have been frustrating at times and would have required the G&P investor to control his emotions via discipline and patience, the strategy had very enviable performance for the 1966–2015 period.

The score of this game is the G&P strategy's return versus the B&H strategy's return. The on-going result of the live test for anyone to see will be documented in real-time via email beginning November 2017. To be included in the free email distribution, send an email to: harrisjohnk@hotmail.com The live test should be of interest to many—individual investors, financial advisers, professional money managers, market strategists, market technicians, financial journalists and the academic community.

Beginning November 2017, will the G&P strategy achieve higher returns and take lower risk than the B&H strategy for the years to come? Time will tell.

Suppose an investor chooses to use the G&P strategy after watching its performance during the live test for, say, two years. After she takes this step (with some portion of her stock portfolio), further suppose the G&P strategy performs even half as well as it did during the back-tested period. Such performance would grow and protect her wealth splendidly.

If sufficient demand develops, you will have the option to subscribe to my low-cost service to receive email alerts on the days that a G&P buy or sell signal occurs. These alerts would be sent at 2:00 pm Eastern time, two hours before the close of trading, so that the trade can be executed that day. If interested, see the website for details.

To actually use the G&P strategy when a buy signal occurs, buy one of the ETFs listed in the bottom part of Table 1-3 (p. 16)—paying an online commission of less than $10 for the trade regardless of its size—and hold it until the next sell signal occurs. At that time, sell the ETF and hold the proceeds in cash or Vanguard's Short-Term Bond ETF (symbol BSV).

For aggressive G&P investors, the Proshares Short S&P 500 ETF (symbol SH) can be bought during sell signals, rather than holding cash or BSV. Likewise during buy signals, ProShares Ultra S&P 500 ETF (symbol SSO) can be bought rather than one of the low-cost S&P 500 ETFs.

Always keep two points in mind. First, when deciding whether to invest in an ETF, be sure to read the current prospectus before investing. Second, it is *not* desirable to apply the **G&P** signals to individual stocks, because they are much more volatile than ETFs.

High Stock Valuations

High stock valuations don't necessarily indicate the S&P 500 is ready to decline. A recent article[6] gave helpful insight about today's high stock valuations:

> Price/earnings ratios are volatile, but consider the more stable long-term valuation indicator popularized by Nobel Prize winning economist Robert Shiller. His metric, the **cyclically adjusted price/ earnings [CAPE] ratio**, is based on the S&P 500's current price divided by its average earnings over the past 10 years adjusted for inflation. It currently [July 31, 2016] stands at 27.1, well above its long-term average of about 16.
>
> Today's valuation falls into the top tenth of historical observations, based on data since the 1880s. When the CAPE is in the top [tenth of historical observations], the S&P 500 subsequently averages [a poor mean return of] about 4% annually for the next 10 years. The upshot: While [the CAPE is] not a short-term market-timing tool, such stock-market valuations often have led to worse returns a decade later.

Appendix D discusses the CAPE in more detail; see pp. 107–108.

Worldwide Ultra-Low and Even Negative Interest Rates

A recent Associated Press article gives a good summary of the current interest rate situation:[7]

> "Record low interest rates were meant to be a temporary response to the global financial crisis.
>
> But eight years later, rates are still near zero or even below in much of the developed world, and some experts are warning of long-term side effects: a hit to pension savings, pressure on banks and possible booms and busts in stock markets and real estate.
>
> …

---

6   Steven Russolillo, "Stock Values Flash a Warning Sign," *The Wall Street Journal* (August 15, 2016), p. C1.

7   *Tulsa World* (August 14, 2016), p. E2.

Here's a [Q&A] look at how we got here and what ultra-low interest rates mean for people.

How did rates get so low? Central banks in the U.S., Europe and Japan are keeping their benchmark interest rates at zero or just above in response to financial crises and weak economic growth. To further reduce borrowing costs, central banks have purchased [a staggering $25 trillion] in mortgage, corporate and government bonds. This increased demand for bonds drives up their prices and lowers their yields, or interest rates. The European Central Bank has been so aggressive as a buyer that German 10-year bonds now yield slightly less than zero, meaning that rather than paying interest when it borrows for a decade, the German government earns a small profit.

Why did central banks cut rates so much? The idea is to stimulate economic growth and job creation by cutting borrowing costs for businesses and consumers, making it easier to buy things and invest in new production. They lower returns on savings accounts and other ultra-safe investments and are intended to push people toward riskier but potentially more profitable ones, such as stocks, bonds and real estate....

What is the downside? Some experts warn [that low interest rates] can encourage investors looking for higher returns to bid up too much the price of riskier investments. That can lead to a "bubble" in that market that is at some point followed by a crash. Economists at Germany's Commerzbank warned house prices in Germany 'look increasingly like a bubble.'

...

Is that the only risk? No, low interest rates also mean that people's savings won't grow as much over the years. Central banks have cut rates to encourage savers to spend or invest, but it could also have the opposite effect. People or companies who see their savings are not growing as much as hoped due to lower returns could put more money aside, not less....

When does all this end? Interest rates were supposed to be slowly raised from record lows as economies started to recover. But that's not happening. Even in the U.S., where the economy is growing slowly but steadily, the Fed has been very cautious in raising its key rate, making only one quarter-point [increasing the range] to 0.25–0.50 percent.

Some economists say that weaknesses in the global economy may mean that the normal level of interest rates is lower than it used to be—and central banks have to take that into consideration. If they don't, they wind up setting rates that are higher than the economy can bear."

Summary and Conclusions for Part Two

The **G&P** strategy engages in market timing, thereby challenging the notion that the S&P 500 segment of the stock market is efficient. Based on back-testing for the 1966–2015 period, the mean number of trades was 4.6 per year. Five statistics summarize the **G&P** strategy's historical return-and-risk performance versus the **B&H** strategy:

Performance Summary, 1966–2015

	G&P Strategy	B&H Strategy
◆ Mean annual return	15.5%	11.1%
◆ Calendar years required to recoup the maximum loss	2	7
◆ Number of years having a negative return	6	11
◆ Worst annual return	−5% (1974)	−37% (2008)
◆ Total accumulation, 1966–2015 (from $1,000 initial investment)	$975,836	$101,361

In comparison to the **B&H** strategy, the **G&P** strategy generated "sleep well" performance indeed.

Using a biblical context, the **G&P** strategy is David doing battle with Goliath, the **B&H** strategy. The battle began in November 2017. The battle is being tracked via emails. If you want to be included in the free email distribution list, let me know: harrisjohnk@hotmail.com David isn't just trying to force Goliath to have an attitude adjustment; David is trying to kill Goliath—which academicians tell us would take many decades. During this long period, there will be mutual hostility between David and Goliath. If in the end David does kill Goliath, the vast majority of financial experts who believe market timing is a fool's errand will be wrong.

Because the performance statistics for the **G&P** strategy resulted from back-testing for the 1966–2015 period, readers are urged to be skeptical about the future performance of the **G&P** strategy. Of course, past performance of any investment strategy is no guarantee of its future results. Nonetheless, you may desire to track what happens going forward by joining the free email distribution list.

I praise the Lord for both the **B&H** strategy and the **G&P** strategy. I feel blessed being able to tell you about them.

I welcome your comments and questions on Chapters 3–5 at harrisjohnk@ hotmail.com

PART THREE

My Spiritual Journey[1]

My spiritual journey has four distinct segments (so far). Segment 1: The 40-year period, the Fall 1957 to July 19, 1997. Several events during that time indicate my interest in stock market timing. Segment 2: My life-changing spiritual experience on July 20, 1997. Segment 3: The 19-year period after my spiritual experience, ended October 14, 2016 (the date this book was published). Segment 4: The live test of the G&P strategy, beginning October 14, 2016.

Chapter 6 describes Segments 1 and 2. Chapter 7 describes Segment 3. My spiritual journey is a testimony to God's plan for my life. That plan first became apparent to me on July 20, 1997. The subsequent 19 years have been filled with personal ups and downs. Via the live test that began October 14, 2016, time will tell if the G&P strategy—Segment 4—is an up or a down.

---

1 Some readers of this book played a role in my spiritual journey. (1) They reviewed my book manuscripts, (2) They were participants in my "God and the Stock Market" classes and/or (3) They are friends who heard me tell various parts of my spiritual journey. That journey is reported in full in Part Three.

Chapter 6

◇◇◇◇◇◇◇◇◇◇◇◇◇◇◇◇

My Life-Changing Spiritual Experience

Chapter Overview

On July 20, 1997, I had what I believe was a life-changing spiritual experience. It concerned God and the stock market (specifically the S&P 500). In this chapter, I describe the experience in detail.

Several events in my life preceded the spiritual experience. The most important of these was I became a evangelical Christian on July 5, 1987. Also important, in Spring 1997 I took disability retirement from my position as a professor of accounting at the University of Tulsa. My disability, which occurred at age 55, was due to my vision problem coupled with the advent of computerized classrooms at the University of Tulsa.

The **G&P** strategy's objective is to **grow** and **protect** the investor's wealth by achieving higher returns and taking lower risk compared to the **B&H** strategy. Obviously, both strategies focus on money. In his tape series, "Mastery of Materialism," John MacArthur, pastor of Grace Community Church in Sun Valley, California, emphasized: "More is said in the New Testament about money than heaven and hell combined; five times more is said about money than prayer; and while there are 500 plus verses on both prayer and faith, there are over 2,000 verses dealing with money and possessions." In his book *The Word on Finances*, Larry Burkett stated that the number of Bible references to money is second only to the subject of love.

I believe, however, that the money or wealth aspect of my historical stock market research is only the tip of the iceberg. The rest of the story is the life-changing spiritual experience—hereafter simply referred to as spiritual experience—I had on July 20, 1997 (described below), and its 19-year aftereffects (described in Chapter 7).

Background Events

Several events occurred during the 1957–1997 period that indicate my interest in stock market timing has been a part of my life for almost 60 years.

Fall 1957. In the mid-1950s, when I was age 13, my grandmother put $1,000 in a growth-oriented mutual fund in my name. At my mother's insistence, I kept a record of the fund's quarterly performance. I watched the fund rise some 30% by the end of June 1957. Then, from July 15 to October 22 of 1957, the S&P 500 fell 20.7%, and the fund had an even larger decline. At that time I remember having a thought I couldn't articulate until the early 1970s: There must be a better way to invest in the stock market than buying-and-holding mutual funds.

Early 1970s. I read two articles in *Barron's* by Martin Zweig, a regular panelist for many years on the "Wall Street Week" TV program. Zweig's articles used historical relationships to develop rules for stock market timing. During that time, Zweig and I corresponded and talked by phone a couple of times. However, it became clear to me in the following years that Zweig's various market-timing rules were not very effective.

December 1972. Regarding my interest in stock market timing, I wrote a letter to TIAA-CREF, which is a large investment company. (I still have a copy of that letter and the company's reply.) As a new participant in the retirement program administered by TIAA-CREF, I asked why those under age 60 were not allowed to make transfers to and from the CREF Stock Fund, the company's only equity fund at the time. The company's reply stated that the policy of not permitting transfers was "somewhat paternalistic" and TIAA-CREF was not "ready for an arrangement which encourages participants to try to guess the [stock] market by trying to time transfers." Sixteen years later (1988), TIAA-CREF changed its policy to allow such transfers.

Late 1970s. A friend gave me a copy of Yale Hirsch's *Stock Trader's Almanac*. It provided a fascinating look at stock market history that was all new to me.

Early 1992. I was on sabbatical from the University of Tulsa. I spent a few months studying at Stanford's Graduate School of Business. During that time, Srikant Datar, an accounting professor, and I became friends. Srikant had just been selected to co-author Charles T. Horngren's popular textbook, *Cost Accounting: A Managerial Emphasis*. Srikant has been the lead author of the book since 2003.

November–December 1996. On November 26th, I talked to Louise Brown, a friend. She said something like, "The stock market seems quite high now. You're a business-school professor, so tell me: When should I sell my tax-deferred stock funds and put the proceeds into a money market fund for safety?" I chuckled and said, "Unfortunately, nobody knows the answer to that question."

Later that same day, I read an interesting article in *USA Today*, "Dauntless Dow: Too Far, Too Fast?" Citing the work of James Stack of *InvesTech Research,* the article said the Dow Jones Industrial Average (the Dow) had risen 20% or more for two consecutive calendar years six times since 1900. And it appeared that 1995–1996 would be the seventh time (which did happen).

The point of the article was that the year following the two stellar years had *always* been very weak. In fact, two of the following years were 1929 and 1987, when the two biggest crashes in the Dow's history occurred. The other four following years all had losses, ranging from 17% to 49%. The conclusion from history was clear to me: 1997 was a time for extreme caution. Under the terms of my disability contract, my university salary was reduced by 40%. So, increasing or even maintaining the stock portion of my portfolio did not seem prudent.

Here's how the Dow performed for the following six years:

1997	23%
1998	16%
1999	25%
2000	−10%
2001	−7%
2002	−17%

After the two consecutive stellar years, 1995–1996, *three more stellar years occurred in 1997, 1998 and 1999*! In tracking this situation at that time, I was stunned to see that the preceding cases were nothing like what happened in the late 1990s. In fact, 1995–1999 was the best performing five-year period in the Dow's then 100-year history! That is, it was different this time. Personally, I missed out on what could have been some very strong growth in my portfolio. Hey, timing is everything!

In a speech on December 5, 1996, then Federal Reserve Chairman Alan Greenspan used the phrase "irrational exuberance" to raise a question about the level of stock prices at that time. After reading Greenspan's speech on the Internet, I couldn't help but wonder if the correct answer to Louise's question was: "Sell your stock funds now."

> I became a born-again Christian on July 5, 1987. (The Bible explains the meaning of "born again" in John 3:1-8).
>
> For the spring semester of 1997, I was on medical leave from my faculty position at the University of Tulsa. I was awaiting the decision on my application for disability retirement, which related to my vision problem coupled with the advent of computerized classrooms at the University of Tulsa. I was granted disability retirement in May 1997. At the time I was 55 years old.
>
> I had planned to work 10 more years before retiring. Under the terms of my disability contract, my university salary was to be reduced by 40%; this meant my retirement next egg would be much smaller than I had planned it to be.
>
> During the process of preparing the application for my disability retirement, Dr. Dick Mills, my ophthalmologist, said: "John, God obviously has something else in mind for your life." At that time I was too dejected about leaving my faculty position to believe what he told me. Now I believe Dr. Mills' statement was prophetic.

January–June 1997. A few months before my disability retirement began, I felt moved to study stock market history in earnest due to my personal circumstances. I thought the study might help me cope with the sharply reduced level of income I would receive under the disability retirement program. I wanted to "grow and protect" my retirement nest egg in a prudent way. I knew there was considerable risk associated with having, say, 50% of my nest egg in the stock market—especially because—like Louise Brown, James Stack and Alan Greenspan—I thought stock prices seemed unreasonably high at that time. However, I also knew financial advisers probably would recommend that I should have at least half of my nest egg in the stock market. For the next three years (1997–1999), history now tells us the S&P 500 had fabulous annual returns of 33.4%, 28.6% and 21.0%, respectively.

Since I didn't know how to prepare Microsoft Excel spreadsheets at the time, Jim Payne (then a faculty member at the University of Tulsa), took formulas I gleaned from the finance literature (as well as some I developed myself) and prepared computer printouts for me to study. I recall that in January 1997, Jim told me a powerful story. After entering formulas and sorting about 650 monthly closing values for the S&P 500, Jim said that 15-minute task would have taken all day on a large company's mainframe computer in 1981! That example motivated me to learn Excel.

I've taken undergraduate and graduate courses in finance, but—believe it or not—I've never taken a college course in Investments.[2] Early on in my study of market timing, I realized the investor needs to sell stocks before he could be in a position to buy them back later at lower prices. That is, if an investor had the ability to identify stock market bottoms (ideal times to buy stocks) but had no cash available to invest then, the buying opportunities would be wasted. My thinking can be expressed as "Sell, then buy lower," which is distinctly different than the age-old advice of "Buy low, sell high."

In April 1997, Srikant Datar, an accounting professor now at the Harvard Business School, was in Tulsa to speak at a conference. I told him I was studying stock market history, and he gave me considerable encouragement to continue that activity. His encouragement has been very helpful ever since.

As my study evolved into research that continued over the years, I concluded *investors have nowhere else to look for guidance except history.* Because human nature never changes, people tend to have repetitive patterns of behavior:

> Ecclesiastes 1:9 (NIV)
> *What has been will be again,*
> *what has been done will be done again;*
> *there is nothing new under the sun.*

> Ecclesiastes 3:15 (Amplified Bible):
> *That which is, already has been,*
> *and that which will be already has been,*
> *for God seeks what has passed by*
> *(so that history repeats itself).*

After doing research on stock market timing during the first six months of 1997, I was on the brink of concluding that, over the long-term, no strategy could earn a higher return and take the same or lower risk than the B&H strategy. In what I thought would be my final attempt in studying market timing, I decided to examine seven indicators (formulas) that I had not investigated before. The seventh formula—my own idea of how to measure investors' greed—was based on a *Barron's* article I had read a couple of months earlier. I called that formula "Indicator X."

In considering whether the results of the calculations from the seven formulas were going to fit on the computer printout, I realized there would be enough blank space to accommodate the output of an eighth formula. I didn't have one in mind but, at that moment, what seemed like a strange

---

2   Not taking a college course in Investments is a blessing in disguise, because I wasn't taught that the efficient market theory is true. Chapter 2 discusses that theory (pp. 24–25).

idea for that formula came to me. I called the eighth formula "Indicator Y." I thought of Indicator Y as sort of a joke, just something to fill the space on the printout. Later on I realized that the idea represented by Indicator Y is somewhat analogous to the notion of conducting an agility drill in youth soccer with a football! That is, it seemed to make no sense at first. (That analogy is explained in Chapter 7.)

With my "sell first" idea in mind, I had previously gone through my database and highlighted in yellow the high month in each of the S&P 500's market cycles during the January 1943 to June 1997 period. (Later in my research such yellow highlighting became the color red.) Shortly before printing the calculations of the eight formulas, I went through my database again and highlighted in green the low month of each market cycle. This meant yellow and green—indicating the ideal months to sell and buy, respectively—would alternate in the printout.

July 20, 1997. The printout was prepared on Sunday afternoon, July 20, 1997. That evening I had a life-changing spiritual experience—divine intervention in my life—that I believe led Kip Karney (my research partner) and me to try to develop an effective market-timing strategy.

As I started to examine the printout about 9 pm, I focused on the patterns of the indicators for the months highlighted in yellow (the ideal sell dates). At the first sell date (February 1946), I saw that Indicator X had an interesting pattern and, surprisingly, Indicator Y did too! However, I paid little attention to Indicator Y's pattern because that formula had seemed like a strange idea. At the next ideal sell date (June 1948), I saw that Indicators X and Y each had patterns resembling those at the first ideal sell date. I also noticed that both indicators had interesting patterns at the first ideal buy date (October 1946). *I couldn't imagine what was going on with Indicator Y.*

After carefully studying the patterns at the first two ideal sell dates, I moved to the third ideal sell date. In doing so, I paused at the second ideal buy date; Indicators X and Y each had patterns resembling those at the first ideal buy date! Then, I quickly thumbed through the other pages of the printout, pausing briefly at each marked sell date and buy date. *Indicators X and Y had patterns that repeated themselves in many cases.*

At that moment the atmosphere in the room changed markedly to a warm, comforting feeling. I felt God's very strong presence, but there was nothing audible. At that time, I was moved to promise God that, if this was going to be a commercial project and if it was successful, I would give generously from the profits. That giving would go to Christian organizations to help advance the Kingdom of God.

Of course, some people don't believe in God. And some of those who do believe in God might not think He would have any involvement with stock market timing. They might say I didn't really have a spiritual experience at all—it was just my unconscious mind at work. Nonetheless, I do believe the experience happened as I have described it.

Why Me, Lord?

After I told one of my non-Christian friends about my spiritual experience, he asked me: "Why would (or did) God choose you for this research on stock market timing? My short answer was, "Why not me?" I told him that on many occasions in the Bible, as well as after it was written, God has called ordinary people to do extraordinary things.

After thinking more about his question, my long answer to him was a list of six factors that explain why I think I was chosen for this work:

1. I believe the Bible is the inspired Word of God.

2. God wanted to test my faith in connection with the major disappointments of (a) my disability retirement and (b) "going public" with my testimony about my spiritual journey.

3. I developed research and writing skills during my 30-year career as a college professor.

4. As described above, I have had a long-time interest in stock market timing.

5. God gave me sufficient analytical ability to do the research.

6. Because I was on disability retirement, I had plenty of time to do the research.

God's Incredible Attributes

In the days and weeks immediately after my spiritual experience, I thought a lot about three of God's incredible attributes: (1) He is omnipotent, (2) He is omnipresent and (3) He is omniscient. Omnipotent means all powerful, having unlimited authority or influence. Omnipresent means present in all places at all times, which obviously includes the stock market. Omniscient means all knowing: having infinite awareness, understanding and insight.

Since God has these attributes, I felt blessed to be a part of His plan for me. Praise the Lord!

Confidence From Scriptures

In the days and weeks after my spiritual experience, some thoughts from W. Phillip Keller[3] were helpful to me:

---

3   W. Phillip Keller, *A Shepherd Looks at Psalm* 23 (Zondervan, 1970), pp. 119, 122-123.

"In every situation and under every circumstance there is comfort in the knowledge that God's Word can meet and master the difficulty if we will rely on it.

…

And as we comply and cooperate with His [the Holy Spirit's] gentle promptings, a sense of safety, comfort, and well-being envelops us... There is a calm, quiet repose in the knowledge that He is there to direct even in the most minute details of daily living. He can be relied on to assist us in every decision, and in this there lies tremendous comfort for the Christian."

By believing in the Scriptures, I was able to live in a sense of quiet rest.

I sincerely believe God inspired me to write this book. Proverbs 1:5 (NIV) states the basic purpose of the book:

Let the wise listen and add to their learning,
and let the discerning get guidance.

Chapter 7

◇◇◇◇◇◇◇◇◇◇◇◇◇◇

The 19-Year After-Effects
of My Spiritual Experience

Chapter Overview

My spiritual journey after my life-changing experience (July 20, 1997) to October 14, 2016, has been event-filled. I gave my Christian testimony, taught a "God and the Stock Market" class, had several speaking engagements, developed seven market-timing strategies and published two books, *The Wall Street Traffic Light* (January 2008) and this one. There were a few personal peaks and many valleys during the 19-year period.

I have openly stated my Christian worldview in Chapters 6 and 7. I respect the fact that your worldview might be different.

I praise the Lord for the stock-market research He prepared in advance for me to do. I'm eternally grateful, and rest in my faith in God and His sovereignty.

During the year following my spiritual experience, I felt God's strong leading. The following developments occurred then:

◆ Based on several days of analysis immediately after July 20, 1997, I determined that—to my amazement—Indicator Y was, in fact, intuitive. It is a measure of investors' fear. My analogy that the idea represented by this indicator is like conducting an agility drill in youth soccer with a football can be considered apt. That's because such a seemingly strange drill could reveal which players move the quickest to the football as it takes unpredictable bounces (in contrast to the more predictable bounces of a soccer ball). That quickness, which might not be as apparent in a drill with a soccer ball, could help identify some less-outstanding youth players who have the potential to play college soccer. In other words, the drill would not be strange. It would have a useful purpose after all.

◆ I thought a lot about the connection between God and the stock market. I was comforted to find this Scripture: *"To these four young men [Daniel, Hananiah, Mishael, and Azariah] God gave knowledge and understanding of all kinds of literature and learning."* (Daniel 1:17, NIV) I believed that, since God gave those men knowledge and understanding of all kinds of literature and learning, He perhaps had given (was giving or would give) me knowledge and understanding of stock market timing.

◆ I developed a "God and the Stock Market" class and taught it weekly at my church in August 1997. About 15 people attended the first few weeks; however, only four continued to attend the class in early 1998. We ended the class a few months later. Having put a lot of time in teaching the class and having risked the vulnerability that went along with sharing my spiritual experience with a group, I experienced discouragement, confusion and embarrassment. I felt my credibility was low and wished many, many times that I had not told anyone about my spiritual experience. I never doubted that the spiritual experience had happened, but I thought I might have misinterpreted its true meaning.

In July 1998, I again felt God's leading. This time I was moved to give my testimony about the spiritual experience that had occurred a year earlier. I did so at my church on the evening of August 17, 1998. About 25 people were there. I covered the material presented above and read several Scriptures that I believe were applicable to my spiritual experience. Those Scriptures focused on two main themes.

1. **Human nature never changes**. It is clear through the centuries that human nature doesn't change. In regard to my research, this means that buyers and sellers of stocks tend to repeat their patterns of behavior. I identified four types of those historical patterns in of my book, *The Wall Street Traffic Light*: A years, B years, C years and Tier 2 years. The findings of that research reveal statistically a truth that the Bible addresses in Ecclesiastes 1:9 (NIV) and Ecclesiastes 3:15, (Amplified Bible); these Scriptures are on p. 65. I believe these patterns demonstrate the truth of those Scriptures about human nature never changing.

2. **Revealing things seen and unseen**. An example of something seen was God parting the Red Sea so the Israelites, en route to their promised land, could escape the pursuit of Pharaoh and his army. (Exodus 14:21-29, NIV) An example of something unseen was God inspiring the prophets Isaiah and

Daniel to write books that are in the Bible—the inspiration itself was unseen at the time the books were written, whereas the books themselves are now seen. In people's minds, *"He [God] reveals deep and hidden things."* (Daniel 2:22, NIV) I believe God led me to be privy to or discover nine stock market timing strategies that were unseen but are now seen; they are discussed later in this chapter.

Following my Christian testimony in August 1998, some of those present wanted me to restart the "God and the Stock Market" class. When interest had waned a few months earlier, I thought I would never teach the class again. However, I consented to restart the class in October 1998. About 20 people attended. By early 1999, only four people continued to attend the class—the same ones who were there a year earlier. (Hmm, human nature never changes!) We ended the class a few months later; the feelings of discouragement, confusion and embarrassment I experienced a year earlier had returned—but this time they were stronger.

In January 2000, I again felt God's strong leading. As a result, I taught the "God and the Stock Market" class two more times (March and April 2000). More than 40 people attended the March class and my presentation was well received. However, less than half the attendees came to the April class. As a result, I became discouraged again and chose to end the class at that time.

In November 2000, I wrote an article, "January's Child," which was published in the December 25, 2000 issue of *Barron's*. (*Barron's* is published weekly on Monday, even when that day is a holiday.) Hmm...my article was in the Christmas Day issue. Since I had no say about when the article would appear, I believed that God was providing me encouragement to continue my research on stock market timing. Although the forecasting model set forth in my article leaves a lot to be desired, a part of that model—whether the S&P 500's price change for January was positive or negative—became an important component of the WSTL model.

In July 2001, I again felt God's leading. This time I was moved to begin using "The Wall Street Traffic Light" as the name for the stock market commentaries I had been emailing to some friends every month or so since February 2000.

In August 2001, I asked four or five Christian friends to provide me counsel. (One came from Houston to participate in this activity.) They advised me to continue doing research on stock market timing but, for the foreseeable future, to only share my research findings with my friends. They believed, in due course, God's plan for the research would be revealed.

In March 2006, I thought my book manuscript was essentially finished and ready to submit to publishers. I thought I would land a book contract soon. As a result, I asked a pastor at my church to conduct a brief Sunday evening service dedicating my book to the glory of God. About 25 people attended. To my surprise and disappointment, I was about to begin 20 grueling months of rewriting before my book manuscript was actually finished in November 2007!

When I completed the development of the WSTL model in February 2006, I realized that Indicators X and Y would *not* be components of it. God really surprised me there! The indicators were intellectually stimulating—thereby keeping me engaged in the research—but were not useful for forecasting the S&P 500's future direction.

In the second half of 2006, my book was rejected by several leading (and some not so leading) publishers. One of the rejections came from the trade division (as distinguished from the textbook division) of Prentice Hall. From 1982 to 2012, Prentice Hall published my popular *Student Guide*, which accompanies the world's leading *Cost Accounting* textbook. It was a big disappointment for me not to land a book contract with either Prentice Hall, McGraw Hill or Wiley.

In January 2007, I decided to do a major rewrite and then self-publish. The book was published in January 2008. I knew that self-publishing has major financial and author-control advantages—*if* the book could clear the formidable marketing hurdle.

The book had a companion website (no longer in existence). The website was free for two reasons:

1. The Christian's salvation is a free gift from God.

2. The firms and financial advisers connected with Wall Street tend to charge investors unreasonable fees (that is, I think many of their services are non-value added).

Through several speaking engagements and word of mouth, I sold 350 books during January 2008–February 2009. Then, sales dried up; less than 10 books were sold during March 2009–December 2009. The sales slump exactly coincided with the time I was diagnosed with and treated for prostate cancer.

In mid-December 2009, I again felt God's leading. During the next six weeks I had two items published in *Barron's*. In one item, the WSTL sell signal (at the close of trading on January 29, 2010; S&P 500 1073.87) was announced—only the 33rd sell signal during 1935–2010—along with my website address. Under the WSTL model, the buy signal would occur in 2010, no later than the end of November. If the S&P 500 was below 1073.87 at the time of the buy signal, 2010's trade would be profitable; if it was above 1073.87, the trade would be unprofitable.

My website underwent significant improvement from mid-December 2009 to mid-February 2010. There were many indications to me during this period that book sales would kick into high gear in the next few months. For example, my website had 1,625 visitors for November 2009, but there were 27,238 visitors from January 30th to February 13th! Nonetheless, book sales were far below my expectations.

My View This Side of Heaven

I believe God and the stock market are an integrally intertwined combination of subject matter, and I believe I've been highly favored by God. I believe I was able to write this book because of the gifting God gave me. While my hands actually wrote the book, the task was accomplished by God working through me. A related Scripture, which puts the G&P strategy's intended purpose in the correct context, is Deuteronomy 8 entitled "Do Not Forget the Lord," particularly 8:17-18 (NIV):

> *You may say to yourself, "My power and the strength of my hands [and my mind] have produced this wealth for me." But remember the Lord your God, for it is he who gives you the ability to produce wealth, and so confirms his covenant, which he swore to your forefathers, as it is today.*

These verses speak to the grow-and-protect strategy's intended purpose. I am blessed to have been able to write this book.

Praise the Lord!

Nine Market-Timing Strategies, 1997-2016

Up to this point, Chapters 6 and 7 have mentioned/described four market timing strategies. Table 7-1 lists them (numbers 1, 2, 3 and 5), indicates their source and tells their outcome. Three of these strategies have failed, and one was never completed. These four strategies were big setbacks in my spiritual journey.

Table 7-1 lists five other market timing strategies:

4. TIAA Real Estate Fund

6. Value Line's Median Appreciation Potential (MAP)

7. S&P 500's reversion to the mean

8. Investing in Good and Bad Times (GBT)

9. Grow-and-protect (G&P) Wealth

Appendix E (pp. 111–122) gives details about numbers 3, 4, 6 and 7. Appendix F (pp. 123–130) describes number 8. Chapters 3–5 explained number 9.

Table 7-1
Nine Market-Timing Models, 1997–2016

Description (1)	Source (2)	Outcome (3)
1. A weak year immediately follows two stellar years	James Stack, InvesTech, reported in an article: "Dauntless Dow: Too Far, Too Fast?" *USA Today* (November 26, 1996).	Model failed: 1997, 1998, 1999
2. Indicators X and Y: X = the percentage change in the S&P 500 from last month's low to the current month's high Y = the percentage change in the S&P 500 from the current month's low looking back to the preceding month's high	My own work	Model never completed
3. Refined January Barometer: The S&P 500's change for January as a predictor of the ensuing 11 months	My own work published in Barron's: "January's Child." (December 25, 2000).	Model failed 7 times in 15 years (2001–2015)
4. TIAA Real Estate Fund	My own work	Model succeeded: 2004–2016 and counting
5. The Wall Street Traffic Light (WSTL)	My own work, self-published book (2008)	Model failed: 2008, 2010, 2014, 2015
6. Value Line's Median Appreciation Potential (MAP)	My own work	Model never completed
7. S&P 500's reversion to the mean	My own work	Model was too long term
8. Investing in Good and Bad Times (GBT)	Kip Karney's and my own work (proprietary)	Model failed: 2015 and 2016
9. Grow-and-Protect (G&P) Wealth	Kip Karney's and my own work (proprietary)	Model subject to a live test beginning November 2017

Why the G&P Strategy Could Succeed

I have learned a lot from my past strategies that failed or were not completed. That learning permeates the G&P strategy. In fact, one component of the GBT strategy (described in Appendix F) is a key part of the G&P strategy.

Reflections

As noted above, I suffered discouragement, confusion and embarrassment several times after my spiritual experience in July 1997. Now, I am pleased that, soon after my spiritual experience happened, I described it in person and by phone to over 200 Christian and non-Christian friends. To the extent possible in my situation, this Scripture helped guide me: *Trust in the Lord with all your heart and lean not on your own understanding.* (Proverbs 3:5, NIV)

I am in awe of what God has enabled me to do in developing the various market-timing models. Through my sometimes-difficult journey, I came to appreciate the ensuing events much more than if I had been able to develop the G&P strategy at or soon after the time of my spiritual experience.

I thank those who (out of love, friendship, faith, curiosity or other reasons) attended my "God and the Stock Market" classes. I thank those who prayed for a good outcome from my research on stock market timing. I thank those who encouraged (and even pestered) me about my research. And, I am thankful for the workbook *Experiencing God* by Henry T. Blackaby and Claude V. King (LifeWay Press, 1990); it has heightened my awareness of God's presence in my life.

I believe God's hand has guided my research and writing on stock market timing. I present the findings to His glory.

Summary and Conclusions for Part Three

I have openly stated my Christian worldview in this book. I respect the fact that your worldview might be different.

I praise the Lord for this work He prepared in advance for me to do. I'm eternally grateful. I rest in my faith in God and His sovereignty. Jeremiah 9:23a and 24a (NIV) speak to me:

> This is what the Lord says: "Let not the wise man boast of his wisdom...but let him who boasts boast about this: that he understands and knows me, that I am the Lord, who exercises kindness, justice and righteousness on earth."

Chapters 6 and 7 describe an almost 20-year journey I went through, which culminated in my writing this book. As a 75-year old, I'm a member of what is called the Silent Generation. But I've certainly not been silent in telling you about the personal peaks and valleys in my spiritual journey.

Like country music songs, Southern gospel songs are a source of wisdom. In thinking about my 1997–2016 spiritual journey, I really relate to two Southern gospel songs:

◆ "I Don't Regret a Mile (I've Traveled for the Lord)" sung by Howard Goodman

◆ "I Wouldn't Take Nothing for My Journey—Now" sung by Howard and Vestal Goodman

If you're a Christian, I'll see you in heaven. Otherwise, my altar call for you is in the following box.

Four spiritual laws are found in the book of Romans—sometimes called the Romans salvation verses:

1. *[F]or all have sinned and fall short of the glory of God.* (Romans 3:23, NIV)

2. *But God demonstrates His own love for us in this: While we were still sinners, Christ died for us.* (Roman 5:8, NIV)

3. *For the wages of sin is death, but the gift of God is eternal life in Christ Jesus our Lord.* (Romans 6:23, NIV)

4. *That if you confess with your mouth, "Jesus is Lord," and believe in your heart that God raised him from the dead, you will be saved.*
   For it is with your heart that you believe and are justified, and it is with your mouth that you confess and are saved. (Romans 10:9-10, NIV)

A complement to the Romans road to salvation is what Jesus said in John 14:6 (NIV); *"I am the way and the truth and the life. No one comes to the Father except through me."*

According to Revelation, the last book in the Bible, the end of the world will only happen once. Time it carefully! Also, St. Augustine's insight about the element of timing is critical: "God has promised forgiveness to my repentance, but He has not promised tomorrow to my procrastination."

Ponder missionary Jim Elliott's famous words about salvation and eternal life: "He is no fool who gives [up] what he cannot keep to gain what he cannot lose." That is, what cannot be kept is a sinful life; what cannot be lost after a Christian is saved is eternal life.

Finally, Christians take to heart the beautiful words in the hymn, "My Faith Looks Up to Thee" (verse 1):

> My faith looks up to thee,
> thou Lamb of Calvary,
> Savior divine!
> Now hear me while I pray,
> take all my guilt away,
> O let me from this day
> be wholly thine!

The contents of the box are succinctly captured by God's email to mankind from John 3:16 (NIV):[1]

For **G**od so
L **o** ved the
worl **d** that He gave
Hi **s** only begotten son

that who **e** ver believes in
Hi **m** shall not perish
but h **a** ve
everlast **i** ng
l ife.

Before you read this book, did you spend considerable time reading or listening to items about the stock market? Now that you've read the book, you may have decided to use the **B&H** strategy or (in due course) the **G&P** strategy if it proves itself in its live test. Either way, you can free up that reading and listening time and use it for non-market activities such as worship, family, volunteering and hobbies. As Jesus said many times: *Peace be with you.*

I welcome your comments and questions regarding Chapters 6 and 7 at harrisjohnk@hotmail.com

Appendix A

◇◇◇◇◇◇◇◇◇◇◇◇◇◇◇

Saving for Retirement

"The item on which most people don't spend enough is savings.
Savings should be thought of as buying something you want in the future.
For most people, that means living a comfortable life when they retire."

Terrance Odean—University of California, Berkeley
The Wall Street Journal, (January 2, 2015).

A major factor in the eventual size of your retirement nest egg is your savings program over the years. The desirable components of a comprehensive program are saving early in your life, contributing to your employer-sponsored retirement plan and your IRA, and making no withdrawals until you retire. (Unfortunately, many Americans who change jobs cash out their 401(k)s instead of rolling the money over into either an IRA or their new 401(k) plan.) This type of savings program, combined with solid investment returns over the long term and an annual withdrawal rate of, say, 4% when retirement begins, will reduce **longevity risk**—the unpleasant possibility of you (you and your spouse) outliving your retirement nest egg.[1]

The challenge of saving for retirement tends to be greatest for investors in their 20s and 30s, because their retirement is so far in the future. Surveys consistently report that older investors' biggest and most painful mistake was not starting to save sooner than they did. Accordingly, each year contribute as much as you can to your employer-sponsored retirement plan and your IRA. The amount will depend on your financial situation and your commitment to saving. Experts often recommend savings be at

---

1   To predict your life expectancy, go to the "Learning Center" at nmfn.com and click on "Longevity Game."

least 10% to 15% of your annual income, including employer contributions to your retirement plan.

The 4% rule of thumb for withdrawals—recommended by many experts—is a helpful way to set a goal for the minimum size of your retirement nest egg. For example, suppose you want to retire soon and currently have a total accumulation of $600,000. You could withdraw $24,000 per year ($600,000 × 4%) or $2,000 per month. Would that amount, combined with your Social Security benefit and money from other sources, be enough for a comfortable retirement?[2] If not, you should try to save more before retirement. Also, you might work longer. An extra year or two in the accumulating-money-for-retirement phase means an extra year or two less in the withdrawal phase. Delaying retirement by two years could increase the longevity of your retirement savings by more than a decade.[3]

The following example illustrates the importance of saving early in life:[4]

> At age 25, Trisha began putting $4,000 a year into a 401(k), which was matched by her employer. Her account generated a long-term mean annual return of 7%. At age 35, a job change to a small company without a 401(k) plan prevented Trisha from making further 401(k) contributions. She worked for that small company until retiring at age 65, so her 401(k) plan at retirement held only her and her employer's contributions from those first 10 years of employment and their growth.

> Trisha's husband, Scott, at age 35, took his first job with a company that had a 401(k) plan. Until retiring at age 65, he contributed $4,000 a year, which was matched by his employer. His account also generated a long-term mean annual return of 7%.

> Trisha and Scott both reached age 65 in 2015 and retired. By then, Scott had contributed $120,000 ($4,000 × 30 years), his employer had contributed $120,000 and his 401(k) had grown to $779,628. Meanwhile Trisha's comparatively small contributions of $40,000 ($4,000 × 10 years) along with her employer's contributions of $40,000—made decades ago—had grown to $868,053. Trisha's larger accumulation is due to having her money in the financial markets for a longer period of time than her husband. It's never too soon to start saving and investing for retirement.

---

2   As a rule of thumb, financial advisers say, for a comfortable retirement, an individual (a married couple) needs about 70% of her (their) pre-retirement income.

3   Richard A. Ferri, *All About Asset Allocation* (McGraw Hill, 2010), pp. 294–295.

4   Adapted from "A Retirement Primer for Baby Boomers," *The Participant*, TIAA-CREF (November 1992), p. 5.

The tax law in 2016 allows you to make a maximum contribution to your employer retirement plan of $18,000 (or $24,000 if you're 50 or older). Always try to contribute enough to your employer-sponsored retirement plan to qualify for the maximum matching contribution. The phrase "snatch the match" is an apt description of getting this free money for your retirement plan.

Depending on your financial situation, the tax law in 2016 also may allow you to make the maximum IRA contribution of $5,500 (or $6,500 if you're 50 or older). IRAs come in two flavors: Traditional and Roth. To understand the difference between them, to learn if your are eligible and to decide on the flavor for you, consult the Internet and/or your financial adviser.

An effective way to save is to spend less. For suggestions on living well while you save and invest, see *The Motley Fool Personal Finance Workbook* by David and Tom Gardner (Fireside) and *The Millionaire Next Door* by Thomas J. Stanley and William D. Danko (Taylor Trade). Also, you could become a student at Dave Ramsey's Financial Peace University (daveramsey.com/fpu).

Appendix B

◇◇◇◇◇◇◇◇◇◇◇◇◇◇◇◇

Fundamentals of Asset Allocation

This material is helpful to the novice investor as well as other investors who want a review of asset allocation. The main points are as follows:

♦ You will achieve higher returns with lower risk consistently over time with a portfolio that is well diversified across the various asset classes and is rebalanced periodically.

♦ To be well diversified across asset classes, you should not have more than 15% of the stock portion of your portfolio in a small number of individual stocks, including the stock of the company you work for.

♦ Three main factors should guide your asset allocation: (1) your investment goals, (2) your investment time horizon and (3) your tolerance for risk.

♦ Because of the effects of inflation and income taxes as well as the possibility of having a long life, you should not be too cautious about including stock funds in your portfolio.

♦ Target-date funds are a convenient, albeit generally expensive, way to achieve suitable asset allocation as you age.

Diversify Your Portfolio

Asset allocation is deciding on and maintaining a suitable mix of different types of investments in your portfolio [the total of your 401(k)s, IRAs and taxable accounts combined]. The purpose of asset allocation is to spread your investment risk among various asset classes. Investment risk is the combination of market risk, inflation risk, longevity risk, exchange-rate risk as well as other types of risk. Chapter 1 (p. 9) focused on two measures of market risk for the B&H strategy. Inflation risk, longevity risk and exchange-rate risk are defined later in this Appendix. The "other types of risk" are beyond the scope of the fundamentals in this discussion.

There are four main **asset classes**: (1) stocks (both domestic and foreign), (2) real estate investment trusts (REITs), (3) bonds and (4) cash equivalents. Although REITs are stocks of companies that own real estate and pay sizable dividends, they are in a different asset class than stocks. That's because there tends to be low to moderate correlation between the annual returns of REITs and the annual returns of the other types of stocks. That means the annual returns of those two assets classes combined are smoothed out over time. Spreading your investment risk among the four main asset classes is the essence of asset allocation.[1]

An integral part of asset allocation is to be well diversified *within each of the asset classes*. Mutual funds are a popular, convenient but often expensive way to achieve broad diversification. Over 95 million Americans owned mutual funds in 2014; more than 42 million of them had mutual funds in their 401(k)s and IRAs. Broadly diversified index mutual funds (such as an S&P 500 index fund) have become popular since the mid-1990s, primarily due to their low costs.

Suppose stocks comprise 60% of Kent's $100,000 portfolio, or $60,000. To be well diversified, he might distribute the $60,000 to index funds as follows: $45,000 in the S&P 500, $3,000 in U.S. small company stocks and $12,000 in foreign stocks.

Many investors include individual stocks in their portfolios. Without a doubt, it's exhilarating to buy an individual stock that soars and then sell it before a severe decline occurs. That's hitting an investment home run! But the odds of consistently doing that are low. Evaluated as a group, individual investors' holdings of individual stocks underperform the S&P 500—that is, their holdings of individual stocks have lower return and higher risk than the S&P 500—for almost any 5-year period selected.

The negative aspects of investing in individual stocks can be formidable. As an extreme example, think about the pain felt by the many Enron employees, who held a large number of shares of the company's stock in their 401(k)s. When the company went bankrupt in 2001, they suffered a total loss.

Recent studies show that it's not uncommon for employees to have over one-half of their retirement assets invested in stock of the company they work for. If the company prospers over time, that strategy will be highly successful—albeit with high risk. However, as in the Enron example, the strategy can be disastrous. *As a general guideline to help control risk, you should not hold more than 5%–10% of the stock portion of your portfolio in stock of the company you work for.*

If you invest in individual stocks beyond the company you work for, I

---

1   Most experts include other asset classes, such as real estate investment trusts (REITs), precious metals and cash equivalents. To simplify, I limit most of the discussion to two major asset classes: the S&P 500 and bonds.

recommend you use an "investment recreation budget" to control the size of that component of your portfolio. As a guideline, do not allow the total value of this small number of individual stocks—including the stock of the company you work for—to exceed 15% of the stock portion of your portfolio. Staying within that limit means the individual stocks, whether winners or losers, will probably not have a sizable effect on your portfolio's return and risk.

Return, Market Risk and Exchange-Rate Risk

The tradeoff between return and risk is a basic investment concept. In general, the higher the expected return on an investment, the more the risk involved. An investment entails **market risk** to the extent that its value is subject to fluctuation. The greater the possible fluctuations in value, the greater the market risk. Prudent management of risk is critical to investors' financial well-being.

Table B-1 presents return and risk statistics for buying-and-holding five types of investments for 1966–2015. The investments are listed in order according to their market risk, from highest to lowest. Two measures of market risk are indicated in the table: (1) the worst annual return and (2) the volatility of annual returns, measured by the standard deviation. The more returns fluctuate from year to year in relation to an investment's average annual return over a period of years, the larger the standard deviation and the higher the market risk.

Table B-1
Annual Returns in U.S. Financial Markets, 1966–2015

Type of Investment (1)	Annual Return			
	Mean (2)	Best (3)	Worst (4)	Volatility (5)
Small company stocks	15.7%	88.4%	−58.0%	25.2%
Large company stocks (S&P 500 Index)	11.3%	52.6%	−35.0%	17.3%
Long-term corporate and government bonds (50:50 mix, 20-year maturity)	8.2%	41.5%	−8.2%	11.3%
Intermediate-term government bonds (5-year maturity)	7.3%	29.1%	−5.1%	6.5%
Treasury bills (30-day maturity)	5.1%	14.7%	0.0%	3.2%

Source: *Stocks Bonds Bills and Inflation 2016 Yearbook* (Ibbotson Associates).

This history tells us that stocks, with a much higher risk, provide a much higher mean annual return than bonds; and bonds provide a higher mean annual return than 30-day T-bills. Small company stocks provide a much higher mean annual return than the large company stocks comprising the S&P 500.

Longer maturity bonds provide a slightly higher mean annual return than shorter maturity bonds.

Concerning REITs and foreign stocks, they both have return and market risk characteristics similar to those of the S&P 500 over the span of a decade or more. Nonetheless, your portfolio's overall risk is reduced by including REITs and foreign stocks along with U.S. stocks. That's because there tends to be low to moderate correlation among the annual returns of the various types of stocks.

Be aware that foreign stocks entail exchange-rate risk. From the vantage point of the U.S. investor, **exchange-rate risk** results from fluctuations in the value of foreign currencies in relation to the value of the U.S. dollar. For example, U.S. investors who hold Japanese stocks benefit from exchange-rate risk when the yen (the Japanese currency) rises against the U.S. dollar and suffer from that risk when the yen falls against the U.S. dollar.

Inflation and Income Taxes

Many investors underestimate the importance of inflation and income taxes on their portfolios over the long-term. **Inflation** is the decline in the purchasing power of a monetary unit, such as the U.S. dollar. During 1966–2015, the mean annual inflation rate was about 4¼%. At that rate, the purchasing power of an initial balance of $10,000 would fall to $6,718—a decline of 32.8%—in just 10 years! Of course, income taxes generally take a sizable bite out of returns too.

In Table B-1, the mean annual return on long-term corporate and government bonds (a relatively low-risk investment) is 8.2%. That return is called the nominal return, which means it has not been adjusted downward to take into account the effect of inflation. To calculate the real return on those bonds, deduct the inflation rate from the nominal return. Then, to calculate the real return after tax, deduct income taxes from the real return; income taxes themselves are based on the nominal return. In the following example, the investor had a real return after tax of only about one-seventh of the nominal return before taxes.

	Mean Per Year
Nominal return on long-term bonds	8.2%
Deduct: Inflation rate	4.2%
Real return	4.0%
Deduct: Income taxes (assume a total rate of 34% for federal and state taxes): 34% × 8.2% =	2.8%
Real return after tax	1.2%

The message of history over the long term is clear: When inflation and income taxes are considered, only stocks—small company stocks, the S&P 500 and foreign stocks—and REITs have a generous real return after tax. Therefore, you should not be too cautious about including stocks and REITs in your portfolio.

Your Asset Allocation Decision

Determining your asset allocation is both an art and a science. Three main factors should be the guide:

1. Your investment goals

2. Your investment time horizon

3. Your tolerance for risk

Each factor is unique to your situation. In deciding your asset allocation at any given age, the challenge is to balance the conflicting objectives of high return and low risk. Over your lifetime, your asset allocation will need to change from time to time as objectives and circumstances (such as your age) change. It's wise to revisit your asset allocation decision every five years or so, and rebalance your portfolio annually (explained below).

Your investment goals—such as funding a college education or funding retirement—are the basis of your need to take risk. The B&H strategy emphasizes the goal of successful management of your wealth so that you—you and your spouse—will likely have a comfortable income throughout your lifetime. A helpful guideline in planning your retirement income is to know the probability is greater than 95% that you will not outlive your money if you withdraw 4% from your well-diversified portfolio the first year of retirement and, then, adjust that amount upward for inflation each year thereafter.

Your **time horizon** is an estimate of how many years there will be from today through the last year when you withdraw money from your portfolio for living expenses. Your time horizon can last 20 years or more *after* retirement begins. **Longevity risk** is the unpleasant possibility of you—you and your spouse—outliving your wealth. According to the National Center for Health Statistics, the average 65-year-old male in 2016 could expect to live at least 16 more years, while a same-aged female can expect to live at least 19 more years. To predict your life expectancy, go to the "Learning Center" at nmfn.com and click on "Longevity Game."

It is of utmost importance to keep in mind that market declines could interfere with your ability to reach short-term investment goals, while inflation has relatively little impact over shorter time periods. It is necessary to take risk in order to keep pace with inflation.[2] The longer your time horizon, the greater

---

2   *T. Rowe Price Investor* (June 2007), p. 22.

is your ability to take risk, especially since the S&P 500 has risen over virtually any 7-calendar-year period during 1966–2015; see Table 1-2, p. 11. Such risk taking is very important for younger investors, say, those under age 45.

Your **tolerance for risk**, which tends to be difficult to estimate, comprises (1) your willingness to take risk and (2) your ability to prudently take risk. A helpful measure of your willingness to take risk is the maximum percentage decline in the market value of your portfolio that you believe you can withstand. That percentage depends on your fear of loss. *However, be aware that actually experiencing a large loss can be more painful than imagining the distress of that loss.*

Your ability to prudently take risk depends on your time horizon. In general, the shorter your time horizon, the less risk you should take. For example, if you are near retirement or retired, it's prudent to have a smaller portion of your asset allocation in stocks than when you were younger. That way, the likelihood of having to sell a significant amount of stocks at depressed prices is reduced. But a retiree certainly should not avoid stocks entirely. Since the long-term mean annual return of the S&P 500 has been more than double the inflation rate, a retiree having (say) 30% to 40% of his portfolio in stocks helps to reduce longevity risk.

I know intelligent people who will not, under any circumstances, invest in the stock market. I also know intelligent retirees who have almost all of their portfolios in stocks. Neither of these attitudes toward risk is prudent. Because stocks have proven to be the best performing asset class over the decades, investors generally should have a sizable portion of their portfolios invested in the S&P 500. Of course, irreparable harm can be done to a retiree's financial condition if she is too heavily invested in S&P 500 during a severe stock market decline that lasts a couple of years or more.

It is essential to understand that risk comes with the territory in order to meet your investment goals under the conditions of inflation, income taxes and the possibility of having a long life. In other words, stocks—the S&P 500, U.S. small and mid-sized companies and foreign companies—and REITs should account for a significant percentage of your portfolio. But what percentage? The following general guidelines may be helpful:

Time Horizon	Portion of the Portfolio Allocated To				
	S&P 500	U.S. Small-Company Stocks	Foreign Stocks	REITs	Bonds
30 years or more	40% to 60%	5%	20%	15%	0% to 20%
20 years	40% to 50%	0%	10%	15%	25% to 35%
10 years	20% to 35%	0%	5%	10%	50% to 65%

Do those percentages seem high to you? If so, that's because they have a pronounced stock bias to compensate for inflation and longevity risk—two factors investors often underestimate.

Investors range from "conservative" to "moderate" to "aggressive" in their tolerance for risk. Try to put yourself in one of those categories. If you are a conservative investor, then consider the percentages on the low side of the S&P 500 column—even though your natural temperament keeps you from being completely comfortable at those levels. If you are an aggressive investor, the percentages on the high side in that column may be appealing. If you are a moderate investor, choose a percentage near the middle of each bracket in the S&P 500 column.

The reduction in the percentage of stocks from one line in the schedule to the next should be made gradually over several years. That approach prevents you from selling too much stock during a severe or prolonged market decline.

According to a study by the Employee Benefit Research Institute and the Investment Company Institute, many participants in their 401(k) plans were not even close to following the guidelines in the table. Of all the participants in their twenties, 38% had no investments in stock funds and another 22% had 50% or less of their investments in stock funds. Of all the participants in their sixties, 13% had more than 90% of their investments in stock funds.[3] Although employees' 401(k)s would not have comprised employees' entire portfolios in the majority of cases, the study's findings likely indicate that poor asset allocations are prevalent among employees.

To decide on your asset allocation, consider the general guidelines above along with the assistance available at mutual fund companies' websites. Helpful sites include fidelity.com, troweprice.com and vanguard.com For an informed opinion regarding your conclusions or for initial assistance in determining the asset allocation that is right for you, consult a financial adviser.

Rebalance Your Portfolio

You will see in this section that occasionally rebalancing your portfolio increases the return while decreasing the risk. **Rebalancing** means to restore your desired asset allocation in your portfolio. To illustrate, suppose you desire 60% stocks, 20% REITs and 20% bonds. (To simplify this example, cash equivalents are not included in the asset mix.) A year ago the total market value of your portfolio was $60,000. Now it is worth $72,000, primarily due to strong performance of the stock market. The following figures show that your allocation has shifted to 65% stocks, 18% REITs and 17% bonds. To restore your

---

3   Tom Lauricella, *The Wall Street Journal* (December 1, 2004), p. A1.

desired allocation, sell $3,600 worth of stocks, buy $1,440 worth of REITs and buy $2,160 worth of bonds:

	Desired Allocation (one year ago)		Now		Change to Restore Desired Allocation	Desired Allocation (now)	
Stocks	$36,000	60%	$46,800	65%	Sell $3,600 worth	$43,200	60%
REITs	12,000	20%	12,960	18%	Buy $1,440 worth	14,400	20%
Bonds	12,000	20%	12,240	17%	Buy $2,160 worth	14,400	20%
	$60,000	100%	$72,000	100%		$72,000	100%

Note that this rebalancing involved selling a small portion of your stocks, because that asset class performed best for the past year. As a result, you sold stocks at prices higher than they were a year ago. On the other hand, had the portion of your portfolio in stocks declined to 55% instead, you would have bought stocks at prices lower than they were a year ago. In either case, portfolio rebalancing—*which forces you to buy low and sell high*—has been estimated to add 0.3 to 0.4 of a percentage point per year to your portfolio's long-term return, while lowering risk.[4] Of course, when rebalancing your portfolio, it is desirable to keep trading costs and income taxes as low as possible. To do so, try to confine the selling to your stocks, bonds and REITs held in your 401(k) or IRA.

How often should you rebalance your portfolio? Research from highly regarded Ibbotson Associates and others has found that the benefits of rebalancing are nearly identical whether it is done monthly, quarterly, twice a year, or annually.[5] An easy way to remember to rebalance once a year is to do it on or near your birthday. This is an easy way to give yourself a present every year.

Target-date Funds

One of the best known company slogans of all time is: "Go Greyhound...and leave the driving to us." A paraphrase of that slogan describes a target-date fund: "Decide on the year you plan to retire...and leave the asset allocation, diversification within asset classes and portfolio rebalancing to your mutual fund company." That is, if you buy a **target-date fund** and hold it over many years, you dispense with the work of managing your portfolio. The asset allocation is automatically adjusted as the year you plan to retire approaches and is surpassed, to take into account your diminishing tolerance for the risk of investing in stocks. Target-date funds (also known by names such as "freedom funds" and "target retirement funds") are the ultimate in one-stop shopping for individuals who lack knowledge

---

4   Jonathan Clements, *The Wall Street Journal* (December 21, 2005), p. D1.

5   Tom Lauricella, *The Wall Street Journal* (February 14, 2003), p. C13.

about investing, don't think they have time to make good asset allocation and diversification decisions, don't have the inclination to take a hands-on approach, lack self-discipline or want to pay to have it done.

The assets in target-date funds soared 61% in 2015, according to the Investment Company Institute. A main reason for the surge is that 401(k) plans increasingly use target-date funds as the default investment option.[6] However, keep in mind that having a larger percentage of your portfolio in a target-date fund would not be conducive for the B&H strategy. That's because target-date funds include several types of assets in addition to S&P 500 stocks.

To gain further insight, let's look at three target-date funds for the year 2040 and three for the year 2020. The following information is from morningstar.com:

Target-Date Fund	Approximate Allocation to Stocks (as of 7/16)	Estimated Annual Expenses for 2016 (based on total assets in the investor's account)*
Fidelity Freedom 2040 Fund (FFFFX)	99%	0.77%
T. Rowe Price Retirement 2040 Fund (TRRDX)	86%	0.75%
Vanguard Target Retirement 2040 Fund (VFORX)	90%	0.16%
Fidelity Freedom 2020 Fund (FFFDX)	60%	0.67%
T. Rowe Price Retirement 2020 Fund (TRRBX)	61%	0.66%
Vanguard Target Retirement 2020 Fund (VTWNX)	60%	0.14%

*This figure includes the underlying expenses for the combination of funds used in the life-cycle fund.

The allocation to stocks varies among the 2040 funds, which indicates asset allocation is not necessarily an exact science.[7] Fidelity's 2020 fund charged $67 a year per $10,000 of market value in the investor's account (0.0067 × $10,000 = $67), while Vanguard's 2020 fund charged only $14 a year per $10,000. By far, Vanguard has the lowest-cost target-date funds. Is it any wonder Vanguard is the largest mutual funds company?

If you don't want to make asset allocation decisions and do portfolio rebalancing, the annual investment costs of target-date funds are reasonable. However, it is simple and requires little time for even novice investors to achieve their desired asset allocation and diversification, with periodic rebalancing, by using index funds and doing the work themselves. For example, the low-cost S&P 500 index funds listed in Table 1-3 (p. 16) usually charge less than four pennies per trading day for each $10,000 multiple of market value in the investor's account. A bargain indeed!

---

6   Jonathan Clements, *The Wall Street Journal* (April 21, 2007), p. D1

7   Phil DeMuth, *Barron's* (October 17, 2005), p. 45.

In general, target-date funds are expensive. Morningstar tracks over 2,200 target-date funds. The average expense ratio of these funds is 0.90% per year.[8]

---

8   *The Wall Street Journal* (September 6, 2016), p. R5.

Appendix C

◇◇◇◇◇◇◇◇◇◇◇◇◇◇◇

Behavioral Finance[1]

Excerpted from William W. Priest, Steven D. Bleigery and Michael A. Wethoelter *Winning at Active Management: The Essential Roles of Culture, Philosophy and Technology* (Wiley 2016), appeared in *Barron's* (August 22, 2016), p. 21.

"[T]he academic world devised [completed the early development of] modern portfolio theory (MPT) [in the 1960s], promising a simple framework of risk and return and one market portfolio optimal for all investors, as well as the notion of efficient market. Passive investing through index funds was soon to follow.

The empirical record of MPT failed to deliver on its theoretical appeal, however, and by the 1990s financial economists had turned up a great number of theoretical arguments, as well as empirical anomalies in the markets, contrary to what MPT would explain. This body of knowledge, named **behavioral finance**, provides a counterpoint to the simple assumptions of MPT. It pictures a world in which investment decisions are far more complex than cold tradeoffs weighing only numerical measures of risk and return.

Rather than seeing investors as capable of calmly and rationally optimizing risk and reward, behavioral finance recognizes the influence that human emotions and reactions—hopes of earning great profits, fear of difficult choices and inconsistent reasoning about money—exert in economic and investing decisions. Over-reactions to company, market and economic developments are common for

---

1 Professor Richard Thaler, the father of behavioral finance, won the Nobel Prize in Economics (October 2017). He is in partnership with my long-time acquaintance Russell Fuller. Their firm, Fuller & Thaler Asset Management, Inc. was founded in 1993. It's located in San Mateo, CA.

both individual and professional investors and give rise to inefficiencies in share prices."

Appendix D

◇◇◇◇◇◇◇◇◇◇◇◇◇◇

A Note to Those Interested in Technical Analysis

This Appendix contains three tables:

- ◆ D-1 The **G&P** Strategy's Trades, 1966–2015
- ◆ D-2 Data for Technical Analysis
- ◆ D-3 My Research Cited in *Barron's*

The Appendix also discusses three topics that should be of particular interest to those interested in technical analysis:

- ◆ Robert Shiller's cyclically-adjusted price/earnings (CAPE) ratio at bull market tops
- ◆ Volatility Index (VIX) at bear market bottoms
- ◆ Favorable season (November 1–April 30) and unfavorable season (May 1–October 31)

Table D-1 lists the **G&P** strategy's 227 trades for the 1966–2015 period. One-hundred fourteen of the trades were **buy**-to-**sell** and the other 113 were **sell**-to-**buy**. The two types of trades alternate.

Table D-1
The G&P Strategy's Trades, 1966–2015

In total, there were 227 trades.
See the important notes at the end of this table.

| Trade | Signal | Date | S&P 500 | Buy-to-Sell Trade | | Sell-to-Buy Trade | |
				Outcome	Trading Days	Outcome	Trading Days
	Buy	12/31/65	92.43	start date			
#1	Sell	02/24/66	90.89	−1.03%	38		
#2	Buy	03/21/66	89.20			2.49%	18
#3	Sell	04/28/66	91.13	2.16%	27		
#4	Buy	05/23/66	86.20			5.41%	17
#5	Sell	06/08/66	84.93	−1.47%	11		
#6	Buy	07/01/66	85.61			−0.80%	17
#7	Sell	07/21/66	85.52	−0.11%	13		
#8	Buy	08/05/66	84.00			1.78%	11
#9	Sell	08/19/66	79.62	−5.21%	10		
#10	Buy	08/31/66	77.10			3.17%	8
#11	Sell	09/21/66	77.71	0.79%	14		
#12	Buy	10/11/66	74.91			3.60%	14
#13	Sell	10/17/67	95.00	26.82%	256		
#14	Buy	11/21/67	93.10			2.00%	24
#15	Sell	02/27/68	90.53	−2.76%	63		
#16	Buy	03/13/68	90.03			0.55%	11
#17	Sell	02/24/69	98.60	9.52%	211		
#18	Buy	03/20/69	99.84			−1.26%	18
#19	Sell	04/22/69	100.78	0.94%	21		
#20	Buy	06/30/69	97.71			3.05%	48
#21	Sell	07/22/69	93.52	−4.29%	14		
#22	Buy	07/29/69	89.48			4.32%	5
#23	Sell	09/08/69	92.70	3.60%	28		
#24	Buy	09/23/69	95.63			−3.16%	11
#25	Sell	11/19/69	95.90	0.28%	41		
#26	Buy	12/18/69	90.61			5.52%	20
#27	Sell	01/16/70	90.92	0.34%	19		
#28	Buy	02/09/70	87.01			4.30%	16
#29	Sell	03/13/70	87.86	0.98%	23		
#30	Buy	05/21/70	72.16			17.87%	48
#31	Sell	06/10/70	75.48	4.60%	14		
#32	Buy	07/08/70	73.00			3.29%	19
#33	Sell	07/28/71	97.07	32.97%	267		
#34	Buy	08/12/71	96.00			1.10%	11

Table D-1 (continued)
The G&P Strategy's Trades, 1966–2015

Trade	Signal	Date	S&P 500	Buy-to-Sell Trade		Sell-to-Buy Trade	
				Outcome	Trading Days	Outcome	Trading Days
#35	Sell	09/23/71	98.38	2.48%	29		
#36	Buy	11/03/71	94.91			3.53%	29
#37	Sell	11/22/71	90.79	−4.34%	13		
#38	Buy	12/02/71	95.84			−5.56%	7
#39	Sell	03/21/72	106.69	11.32%	76		
#40	Buy	05/12/72	106.38			0.29%	37
#41	Sell	06/26/72	107.48	1.03%	30		
#42	Buy	07/25/72	107.60			−0.11%	20
#43	Sell	09/12/72	108.47	0.81%	34		
#44	Buy	11/01/72	112.67			−3.87%	36
#45	Sell	01/16/73	118.14	4.85%	49		
#46	Buy	02/12/73	116.06			1.76%	18
#47	Sell	03/15/73	114.12	−1.67%	22		
#48	Buy	04/09/73	110.86			2.86%	17
#49	Sell	04/25/73	108.34	−2.27%	11		
#50	Buy	05/21/73	102.73			5.18%	18
#51	Sell	06/04/73	102.97	0.23%	9		
#52	Buy	06/28/73	104.69			−1.67%	18
#53	Sell	08/01/73	106.83	2.04%	23		
#54	Buy	08/28/73	103.02			3.57%	19
#55	Sell	11/12/73	104.44	1.38%	53		
#56	Buy	11/27/73	95.70			8.37%	10
#57	Sell	03/22/74	97.27	1.64%	80		
#58	Buy	04/16/74	93.66			3.71%	16
#59	Sell	05/13/74	90.66	−3.20%	19		
#60	Buy	06/03/74	89.10			1.72%	14
#61	Sell	06/18/74	89.45	0.39%	11		
#62	Buy	07/09/74	81.48			8.91%	14
#63	Sell	07/29/74	80.94	−0.66%	14		
#64	Buy	09/05/74	70.87			12.44%	27
#65	Sell	09/12/74	66.71	−5.87%	5		
#66	Buy	09/17/74	67.38			−1.00%	3
#67	Sell	10/01/74	63.39	−5.92%	10		
#68	Buy	10/07/74	64.95			−2.46%	4
#69	Sell	11/18/74	69.27	6.65%	30		
#70	Buy	12/10/74	67.28			2.87%	15

Table D-1 (continued)
The G&P Strategy's Trades, 1966–2015

				Buy-to-Sell Trade		Sell-to-Buy Trade	
Trade	Signal	Date	S&P 500	Outcome	Trading Days	Outcome	Trading Days
#71	Sell	03/22/77	101.00	50.12%	576		
#72	Buy	04/12/77	100.15			2.10%	13
#73	Sell	07/28/77	98.79	−0.09%	75		
#74	Buy	10/28/77	92.61			6.26%	65
#75	Sell	01/09/78	90.64	−2.13%	48		
#76	Buy	03/10/78	88.88			1.94%	43
#77	Sell	10/20/78	97.95	10.20%	156		
#78	Buy	01/03/79	97.80			0.15%	50
#79	Sell	05/08/79	99.17	1.40%	87		
#80	Buy	06/06/79	101.30			−2.15%	20
#81	Sell	10/09/79	106.63	5.26%	87		
#82	Buy	10/30/79	102.67			3.71%	15
#83	Sell	02/19/80	114.60	11.62%	76		
#84	Buy	03/28/80	100.68			12.15%	28
#85	Sell	12/10/80	128.26	27.39%	177		
#86	Buy	12/22/80	135.78			−5.86%	11
#87	Sell	08/24/81	125.50	−7.57%	169		
#88	Buy	09/11/81	121.61			3.10%	13
#89	Sell	01/13/82	114.88	−5.53%	85		
#90	Buy	02/25/82	113.21			1.45%	30
#91	Sell	05/20/82	114.59	1.22%	59		
#92	Buy	06/11/82	111.24			2.92%	15
#93	Sell	07/08/82	107.53	−3.34%	18		
#94	Buy	08/16/82	104.09			3.20%	27
#95	Sell	04/05/84	155.04	48.95%	416		
#96	Buy	04/24/84	158.07			−1.95%	12
#97	Sell	05/18/84	155.78	−1.45%	18		
#98	Buy	07/26/84	150.08			3.66%	47
#99	Sell	09/13/85	182.91	21.88%	287		
#100	Buy	10/16/85	187.98			−2.77%	22
#101	Sell	10/14/87	305.23	62.37%	504		
#102	Buy	10/19/87	224.84			26.34%	3
#103	Sell	10/28/87	233.28	3.75%	7		
#104	Buy	11/12/87	248.52			−6.53%	11
#105	Sell	11/30/87	230.30	−7.33%	11		
#106	Buy	12/15/87	242.80			−5.43%	11

Table D-1 (continued)
The G&P Strategy's Trades, 1966–2015

Trade	Signal	Date	S&P 500	Buy-to-Sell Trade		Sell-to-Buy Trade	
				Outcome	Trading Days	Outcome	Trading Days
#107	Sell	10/16/89	342.85	41.21%	464		
#108	Buy	12/27/89	348.81			−1.74%	50
#109	Sell	01/16/90	340.75	−2.31%	13		
#110	Buy	02/02/90	330.92			2.88%	13
#111	Sell	04/23/90	331.05	0.04%	54		
#112	Buy	05/08/90	342.01			−3.31%	11
#113	Sell	08/03/90	344.86	0.83%	61		
#114	Buy	08/24/90	311.51			9.67%	15
#115	Sell	09/14/90	316.83	1.71%	14		
#116	Buy	10/01/90	314.94			0.60%	11
#117	Sell	10/11/90	295.46	−6.19%	8		
#118	Buy	10/18/90	305.74			−3.48%	5
#119	Sell	11/19/91	379.42	24.10%	275		
#120	Buy	12/20/91	387.04			−2.01%	22
#121	Sell	10/05/92	407.57	5.30%	199		
#122	Buy	11/27/92	430.16			−5.54%	38
#123	Sell	03/29/94	452.48	5.19%	337		
#124	Buy	04/04/94	438.92			3.00%	3
#125	Sell	05/09/94	442.32	0.77%	24		
#126	Buy	05/26/94	457.06			−3.33%	13
#127	Sell	06/24/94	442.80	−3.12%	20		
#128	Buy	07/15/94	454.16			−2.57%	14
#129	Sell	10/25/94	461.53	1.62%	71		
#130	Buy	12/14/94	454.97			1.42%	35
#131	Sell	07/16/96	628.37	38.11%	400		
#132	Buy	07/31/96	639.95			−1.84%	11
#133	Sell	01/12/98	939.21	46.76%	366		
#134	Buy	02/03/98	1006.00			−7.11%	15
#135	Sell	06/12/98	1098.84	9.23%	90		
#136	Buy	06/29/98	1138.49			−3.61%	11
#137	Sell	07/24/98	1140.80	0.20%	18		
#138	Buy	08/18/98	1101.20			3.47%	17
#139	Sell	08/27/98	1042.59	−5.32%	7		
#140	Buy	08/31/98	957.28			8.18%	2
#141	Sell	10/01/98	986.39	3.04%	22		
#142	Buy	10/16/98	1056.42			−7.10%	11

Table D-1 (continued)
The G&P Strategy's Trades, 1966–2015

Trade	Signal	Date	S&P 500	Buy-to-Sell Trade		Sell-to-Buy Trade	
				Outcome	Trading Days	Outcome	Trading Days
#143	Sell	08/02/99	1328.05	25.71%	198		
#144	Buy	08/17/99	1344.16			−1.21%	11
#145	Sell	09/16/99	1318.48	−1.91%	21		
#146	Buy	10/22/99	1301.65			1.28%	26
#147	Sell	11/23/99	1404.64	7.91%	22		
#148	Buy	12/20/99	1418.09			−0.96%	18
#149	Sell	01/31/00	1394.46	−1.67%	28		
#150	Buy	02/29/00	1366.42			2.01%	20
#151	Sell	09/22/00	1448.72	6.02%	144		
#152	Buy	10/19/00	1388.76			4.14%	19
#153	Sell	11/30/00	1314.95	−5.31%	29		
#154	Buy	01/04/01	1333.34			−1.38%	23
#155	Sell	02/20/01	1278.94	−4.08%	31		
#156	Buy	09/28/01	1040.94			18.61%	150
#157	Sell	03/26/02	1138.49	9.37%	122		
#158	Buy	07/29/02	898.96			21.04%	86
#159	Sell	09/18/02	869.46	−3.28%	36		
#160	Buy	10/11/02	835.32			3.93%	17
#161	Sell	01/27/03	847.48	1.46%	72		
#162	Buy	03/13/03	831.90			1.84%	32
#163	Sell	04/14/04	1128.17	35.61%	274		
#164	Buy	05/25/04	1113.05			1.34%	29
#165	Sell	04/15/05	1142.62	2.66%	224		
#166	Buy	05/04/05	1175.65			−2.89%	13
#167	Sell	09/21/05	1210.20	2.94%	97		
#168	Buy	10/24/05	1199.38			0.89%	23
#169	Sell	07/13/06	1242.29	3.58%	180		
#170	Buy	07/28/06	1278.55			−2.92%	11
#171	Sell	06/21/07	1522.19	19.06%	225		
#172	Buy	08/08/07	1497.49			1.62%	33
#173	Sell	08/15/07	1406.70	−6.06%	5		
#174	Buy	08/17/07	1445.94			−2.79%	2
#175	Sell	10/19/07	1500.63	3.78%	44		
#176	Buy	11/28/07	1469.02			2.11%	27
#177	Sell	12/14/07	1467.95	−0.07%	12		
#178	Buy	01/23/08	1338.60			9.66%	25

Table D-1 (continued)
The G&P Strategy's Trades, 1966–2015

Trade	Signal	Date	S&P 500	Buy-to-Sell Trade Outcome	Buy-to-Sell Trade Trading Days	Sell-to-Buy Trade Outcome	Sell-to-Buy Trade Trading Days
#179	Sell	03/03/08	1331.34	−0.54%	27		
#180	Buy	03/18/08	1330.74			0.05%	11
#181	Sell	06/11/08	1335.49	0.36%	59		
#182	Buy	07/16/08	1245.36			6.75%	24
#183	Sell	09/04/08	1236.83	−0.68%	35		
#184	Buy	09/19/08	1255.08			−1.48%	11
#185	Sell	09/23/08	1188.22	−5.33%	2		
#186	Buy	09/29/08	1106.42			6.88%	4
#187	Sell	10/03/08	1099.23	−0.65%	4		
#188	Buy	10/09/08	909.92			17.22%	4
#189	Sell	11/11/08	898.95	−1.21%	23		
#190	Buy	11/19/08	806.58			10.28%	6
#191	Sell	01/22/09	827.50	2.59%	42		
#192	Buy	03/06/09	683.38			17.42%	30
#193	Sell	05/06/10	1128.15	65.08%	294		
#194	Buy	07/13/10	1095.34			2.91%	46
#195	Sell	08/24/10	1051.87	−3.97%	30		
#196	Buy	09/10/10	1109.55			−5.48%	12
#197	Sell	07/27/11	1304.89	17.61%	222		
#198	Buy	08/08/11	1119.46			14.21%	8
#199	Sell	08/19/11	1123.53	0.36%	9		
#200	Buy	09/14/11	1188.68			−5.80%	17
#201	Sell	10/03/11	1099.23	−7.53%	13		
#202	Buy	10/05/11	1144.03			−4.08%	2
#203	Sell	05/18/12	1295.22	13.22%	156		
#204	Buy	06/12/12	1324.18			−2.24%	16
#205	Sell	07/24/12	1338.31	1.99%	28		
#206	Buy	07/27/12	1385.97			−3.56%	3
#207	Sell	11/08/12	1377.51	−0.61%	70		
#208	Buy	11/29/12	1415.95			−2.79%	14
#209	Sell	06/04/13	1631.38	15.21%	127		
#210	Buy	06/27/13	1613.20			1.11%	17
#211	Sell	08/14/13	1685.39	4.47%	33		
#212	Buy	09/05/13	1655.08			1.80%	15
#213	Sell	12/12/13	1775.50	7.28%	69		
#214	Buy	12/31/13	1848.36			−4.10%	12

Table D-1 (continued)
The G&P Strategy's Trades, 1966–2015

Trade	Signal	Date	S&P 500	Buy-to-Sell Trade		Sell-to-Buy Trade	
				Outcome	Trading Days	Outcome	Trading Days
#215	Sell	09/25/14	1965.99	6.36%	185		
#216	Buy	10/21/14	1941.28			1.26%	18
#217	Sell	12/08/14	2060.31	6.13%	33		
#218	Buy	01/26/15	2057.09			0.16%	32
#219	Sell	06/29/15	2057.64	0.03%	107		
#220	Buy	07/29/15	2108.57			−2.48%	21
#221	Sell	08/19/15	2079.61	−1.37%	15		
#222	Buy	08/25/15	1867.62			10.19%	4
#223	Sell	09/22/15	1942.74	4.02%	19		
#224	Buy	10/07/15	1995.83			−2.73%	11
#225	Sell	11/11/15	2075.00	3.97%	25		
#226	**Buy**	11/27/15	2090.11			−0.73%	11
#227	Sell	12/14/15	2021.94	−3.26%	11		
	Mean			5.65%	90	2.09%	20

Notes:

◆ Dividends are not included in the outcome of each trade. For 1966–2015, the mean annual dividend yield was 3.34%.

◆ *The buy-to-sell trades had the exact same performance as the B&H strategy. That is, the traffic light was green at those times. So, your focus in Table D-1 should be on the sell-to-buy trades—that is, when the traffic light was red.*

◆ Sell-to-buy trades had a mean length of 18 trading days. B&H would receive mean dividends of 0.29% per G&P trade [(18/252) x 3.34%]. G&P would forgo mean dividends of 0.29% per G&P trade—relatively small in regard to the mean gain of 2.09% per G&P trade.

◆ Buy-to-sell trades had a mean length of 92 trading days. Both G&P and B&H would receive dividends of 1.22% per G&P trade [(92/252) x 3.34%].

For the buy-to-sell trades, the mean outcome was a gain of 4.97% per trade in 92 trading days. For the sell-to-buy trades—which are what account for the difference in performance between G&P and B&H—the mean outcome was a gain of 2.05% per trade in 18 trading days. *Note that sometimes the trades occur only a few days apart.*

To tout the G&P strategy's historical performance a bit, consider this example:

	Date	S&P 500	Change
Sell date	02/19/80	114.60	
Buy date	03/28/80	100.68	−12.2%

The actual market top for the February–March market correction was 02/13/80 (S&P 500 118.44) and the correction bottom was 03/27/80 (98.22); the correction was −17.1% [(98.22/118.44)−1]. Therefore, the sell signal captured 71.3% (−12.2%/−17.1%) of the S&P 500 decline. Not bad! This sizable and swift market correction was caused by concerns about interest rates and inflation.

Table D-2 lists over 100 data items used by technical analysts, which by no means is a complete list.

Table D-2
Data for Technical Analysis

Panel 1: Daily Data

Item	Source
◆ S&P 500	Financial press
◆ Dow Jones Industrial Average	Financial press
◆ NASDAQ Composite	Financial press
◆ Russell 2000	Financial press
◆ CBOE Volatility Index (VIX)	Financial press
◆ Gold price	Financial press
◆ S&P 500-to-gold ratio	Financial press
◆ Oil price	Financial press
◆ U.S. Dollar Index	Financial press
◆ S&P 500 price to earnings ratio past 12 months or 12 months ahead; earnings can be based on GAAP, EBITDA or other	Financial press
◆ Golden cross and death cross	Financial press
◆ Advance-decline line	Financial press
◆ Up and down volume	Financial press
◆ Breadth thrusts	James Stack, *InvesTech Research* newsletter
◆ Volume thrusts	James Stack, *InvesTech Research* newsletter
◆ High-Low Logic Index	Norman Fosback, *Stock Market Logic*, p. 79
◆ Baltic Dry Index (BDI)	London-based Baltic Exchange
◆ 12-month trailing price/earnings	Financial press
◆ 12-month forward price/earnings	Financial press
◆ Best days and worst days	H. Nejat Seyhun, research commissioned by Towneley Capital Management, 1994
◆ Elliott Wave Theory	Robert Prechter, *Elliott Wave Financial Forecast* newsletter
◆ TIAA Real Estate Fund	My analysis, unpublished
◆ Negative Leadership Composite	James Stack, *InvesTech Research* newsletter
◆ All clear signal	Austin Pryor, *Sound Mind Investing* newsletter

Table D-2 (continued)
Data for Technical Analysis

Panel 2: Weekly Data

Item	Source
◆ S&P 500	Financial press
◆ Dow Jones Industrial Average	Financial press
◆ NASDAQ Composite	Financial press
◆ Russell 2000	Financial press
◆ CBOE Volatility Index (VIX)	Financial press
◆ Gold price	Financial press
◆ Advance-decline line	Financial press
◆ Up and down volume	Financial press
◆ High-Low Logic Index	Norman Fosback, *Stock Market Logic*, p. 79
◆ Investor sentiment	Investors Intelligence and American Association of Individual Investors
◆ Median Appreciation Potential (MAP)	Value Line Investment Survey
◆ Median P/E ratio (MPE)	Value Line Investment Survey
◆ Initial jobless claims	Department of Labor
◆ Petroleum status report for crude oil and related products	Energy Information Administration
◆ Supply and demand for natural gas	Energy Information Administration

Table D-2 (continued)
Data for Technical Analysis

Panel 3: Monthly Data

Item	Source
◆ S&P 500	Financial press
◆ Dow Jones Industrial Average	Financial press
◆ NASDAQ Composite	Financial press
◆ Russell 2000	Financial press
◆ CBOE Volatility Index (VIX)	Financial press
◆ Gold price	Financial press
◆ Oil price	Financial press
◆ U.S. Dollar Index	Financial press
◆ NYSE short interest ratio	Financial press
◆ S&P 500 dividend yield	Financial press
◆ Margin debt	International Swaps and Derivatives Association
◆ Consumer sentiment	University of Michigan/Reuters
◆ Consumer confidence	Conference Board
◆ Consumer price index (CPI)	Bureau of Labor Statistics
◆ Consumer spending	Commerce Department
◆ Producer price index (PPI)	Bureau of Labor Statistics
◆ Leading economic indicators (LEI)	Conference Board
◆ ISM Purchasing Managers Index (PMI)	Institute of Supply Management
◆ S&P/Case-105 home prices	Standard & Poor's
◆ ISM Service Sector (Business Activity Index)	Institute of Supply Management
◆ Traffic of Prospective Buyers Index	National Association of Home Builders
◆ Builder Confidence Survey	National Association of Home Builders
◆ Durable goods orders	U.S. Census Bureau
◆ Retail sales	Commerce Department
◆ U.S. imports	U.S. Census Bureau
◆ U.S. exports	U.S. Census Bureau
◆ Total vehicle sales	Autodata
◆ Housing starts	U.S. Census Bureau
◆ Existing home sales	National Association of Realtors
◆ New home sales	U.S. Census Bureau
◆ Employment report	Department of Labor
◆ Chicago Fed National Activity Index (CFNAI)	Federal Reserve Bank of Chicago
◆ Cyclical adjusted price earnings (CAPE)	Robert J. Shiller, his website
◆ Future Inflation Gauge	Economic Cycle Research Institute
◆ Economic Surprise Index	Citigroup

Table D-2 (continued)
Data for Technical Analysis

Panel 4: Quarterly Data

Item	Source
◆ U.S. corporate earnings	Financial press
◆ Gross domestic product (GDP)	Department of Commerce
◆ Nonfarm business productivity	Department of Labor

Panel 5: Irregular Data

Item	Source
◆ Federal Open Market Committee (FOMC) minutes	Federal Reserve

Panel 6: Special Studies

Item or Concept	Source
◆ S&P 500	Financial press (e.g., see Exhibit D-3, my research cited in *Barron's* over the years)
◆ Dow Jones Industrial Average	Financial press
◆ NASDAQ Composite	Financial press
◆ Russell 2000	Financial press
◆ CBOE Volatility Index (VIX)	Financial press
◆ Gold price	Financial press
◆ Oil price	Financial press
◆ U.S. Dollar Index	Financial press
◆ Federal Open Market Committee (FOMC) minutes	Federal Reserve
◆ Reversion to the mean	Finance literature (e.g., John C. Bogle, *Common Sense on Mutual Funds* (1999), pp. 225–236
◆ Simple and exponential moving averages applied to any given metric	For example, Jeremy J. Siegel, *Stocks for the Long Run*, 4th Edition (pp. 295–302) and Mebane T. Faber and Eric W. Richardson, *The Ivy Portfolio* (Chapter 7)
◆ Momentum investing	Fund X (FUNDX)
◆ Tactical asset allocation	Finance literature (e.g., John C. Bogle, *Common Sense on Mutual Funds*, pp. 66–67)

Table D-2 (continued)
Data for Technical Analysis

Panel 6: Special Studies (continued)

Item or Concept	Source
◆ January Effect	Robert A. Haugen and Philippe Jorion, "The January Effect Still There After All These Years," *Financial Analysts Journal* (January–February 1996) pp. 27–31.
◆ Favorable and unfavorable seasons	Yale Hirsch, *Stock Trader's Almanac* and James Stack, *InvesTech Research* newsletter
◆ January Barometer	Yale Hirsch, *Stock Trader's Almanac*
◆ 4-year U.S. Presidential cycle	Yale Hirsch, *Stock Trader's Almanac*
◆ Santa Claus Rally	Yale Hirsch, *Stock Trader's Almanac*
◆ S&P 500's Two Consecutive Stellar Years	My analysis, unpublished; see my related study p. 63
◆ Second term U.S. Presidents	Financial press
◆ Republican vs. Democrat U.S. Presidents	Financial press
◆ Three Steps and a Stumble	Edson Gould, Jr.
◆ q-based trading rules	Andrew Smithers and Stephen Wright, *Valuing Wall Street*, Chapter 14
◆ Coppock Guide	James Stack, *InvesTech Research* newsletter
◆ Ulcer Index (a risk evaluation tool)	Peter Eliades, *Stockmarket Cycles* newsletter
◆ The Shemitha	Rabbi Jonathan Cahn, *The Mystery of the Shemitha*
◆ Super Bowl indicator	Bob Stovall
◆ Various ideas of mine	Table D-3, p. 110

Cyclically Adjusted Price-to-Earnings (CAPE) Ratio

Technical analysts worth their salt track the CAPE. From the research of Robert Shiller, a Nobel Prize winning economist, the CAPE's monthly values are available from January 1881 to the present. That's 1,627 months through July 2016—the longest running data series I'm aware of. Because of Shiller's benevolence, this data can be downloaded at no charge.[1] The CAPE value for each month can be sorted from high to low and converted to a percentile to facilitate analysis of the S&P 500's market cycles. What a treasure this data series is!

1 Google Shiller PE Ratio, then click on Shiller PE Ratio-S&P 500 PE Ratio. The graph there gives the big picture of the CAPE's long history.

At this writing (November 8, 2017), the CAPE was 31.62. In its history, the CAPE has been at that level or higher *leading up to major market tops (including the month in which the top occured)* in 34 months, or 2.0% of the time:

	Number of Months	Bull Market Top
1929	1	09/07/29
7/1997–3/2000	33	03/24/00
	34	

The 7/1997–3/2000 case reveals that very high stock valuations can persist a very long time before a bull market ends.[2] The two bull market tops listed are among the most well-known ones in history.

With all the bashing of market timing that goes on, it was refreshing for me to see an article in *The Wall Street Journal* two years ago titled: "Yes, You Can Time the Market."[3] The article explains how the CAPE could have been used for effective market timing during the past 90 years.

Volatility Index (VIX)

Technical analysts worth their salt also track the **volatility index (VIX)**. The VIX is often referred to as the "fear index." In this context, fear refers to concern regarding the near-term possibility of a sizable decline in the S&P 500. If fear is low, the VIX is low. If fear is high, the VIX is high. From its inception on January 2, 1986 to August 31, 2016, the VIX's mean is 20.78 and the standard deviation is 8.72. Since the VIX data fits the pattern of a normal curve well, the mean plus 1.96 standard deviations will specify the level of the upper 2.5% of VIX values:

$$20.78 + 1.96 (8.72) = 37.87$$

The following VIX values at selected bear market bottoms—when fear tends to be very high—are all well above the 37.87 benchmark:

---

2   The long-running bull market that started 03/09/09 also has had high Shiller CAPE values for an extended period.

3   Spencer Jakab, "Yes, You Can Time the Market," *The Wall Street Journal* (August 22, 2014), p. C1.

Bear Market Bottom	VIX
10/19/87	150.19
08/31/98	48.33
09/21/01	48.27
07/23/02	50.48
10/09/02	49.48
11/20/08	80.86
03/09/09	49.68

Favorable Season and Unfavorable Season

Technical analysts worth their salt also track the favorable and unfavorable seasons. In his *InvesTech Research* newsletter, renowned market technician James Stack often updates the performance statistics regarding the S&P 500's **favorable season**—November 1 to April 30—and its **unfavorable season**—May 1 to October 31. This phenomenon was first reported by Yale Hirsch, the long-time editor of the *Stock Trader's Almanac,* in 1986.

Over the 1960–2016 period, the favorable and unfavorable patterns have occurred with a high degree of consistency. To illustrate the significance of the two seasons, let's consider two investors. Investor A invested $1,000 at the beginning of the favorable season in 1960 and only invested the accumulated amount in each favorable six months thereafter. Her initial investment would have been worth $64,026 on April 30, 2016. In contrast, Investor B invested $1,000 at the beginning of the unfavorable season in 1960 and only invested the accumulated amount in each unfavorable six months thereafter. As of October 31, 2015, his total accumulation would have been $2,927. So, the vast majority—($64,026 – $1,000)/[($64,026 – $1,000) + ($2,927 – $1,000)]= (97%)— of the S&P 500's gain since 1960 occurred in the favorable season.

The mean gain for all favorable seasons was 6.9%, with double-digit gains occurring 36% of the time. The mean gain for all unfavorable seasons was 0.9%, with double-digit gains occurring only 13% of the time.

Evidence of My Credentials

Table D-3 provides evidence of my credentials as a stock market historian. Moreover, you have seen numerous examples of my knowledge of the S&P 500's history throughout the book.

Table D-3
My Research Cited in Barron's

(a baker's dozen in chronological order)

1. Michael Santoli, The Trader column, *Barron's* (December 1, 2003), p. MW3.
   - The S&P 500's long winning streaks of 120 trading days or more without a 5% pullback placed in the context of the bull market's length.

2. Michael Santoli, "Dullsville U.S.A.," *Barron's* (July 19, 2004), p. 19.
   - The S&P 500's very low volatility in January–June periods linked to the 4-year U.S. Presidential cycle.

3. Michael Santoli, The Trader column, *Barron's* (August 16, 2004), p. MW3–MW4.
   - Of the 18 years when the S&P 500 reached a YTD low after July 31, 10 saw the year's low occur in August.

4. Michael Santoli, The Trader column, *Barron's* (February 20, 2006), p. M3.
   - The Dow's long winning streaks of 120 trading days or more without a 5% pullback compared to the current streak.

5. Alan Abelson, Up&Down Wall Street column, *Barron's* (October 27, 2008), p. 6.
   - The near-term aftermath in U.S. Presidential election years when the S&P 500 was in a bear market on Election Day.

6. Michael Santoli, The Trader column, *Barron's* (December 29, 2008), p. M5.
   - Years when the S&P 500 fell 10% or more in the October–December quarter typically ushered in a very weak next year.

7. Michael Santoli, Streetwise column, *Barron's* (February 23, 2009), p. 15.
   - Years when the S&P 500 fell 10% or more in January or February had much more downside in the following months.

8. Michael Santoli, Streetwise column, *Barron's* (October 19, 2009), p. 5.
   - The S&P 500's rally in 2009 was remarkably similar to the rally in 1938.

9. Michael Santoli, "Bullish Trends for 2010," *Barron's* (January 4, 2010), p. 11.
   - The S&P 500's near-term prospects when its high for the preceding year occurred in December.

10. Michael Santoli, "Too Beautiful for You," *Barron's* (February 21, 2011), p. 19.
    - The S&P 500's long winning streaks of 120 trading days or more without a 5% pullback placed in the context of the bull market's length.

11. Michael Santoli, "Enjoying a Low-Volume Levitation," *Barron's* (March 28, 2011), p. 21.
    - Years when the S&P 500 did not close lower than the preceding year's closing high had an average return far better than the average return for all years.

12. Michael Santoli, "Awaiting September's Performance," *Barron's* (September 5, 2011), p. 11.
    - The S&P 500's June–August performance as a predictor of September.

13. Michael Santoli, The Trader column, *Barron's* (January 2, 2012), p. M3.
    - Years when the S&P 500 total was in the range of −5% to +5% had a positive tendency for the next year, but sometimes with nastiness involved.

Appendix E

✕✕✕✕✕✕✕✕✕✕✕✕✕✕

Details About Four Market-Timing Models

This appendix discusses the following models from Table 7-1 (p. 74):

3. Refined January Barometer
4. TIAA Real Estate Fund
6. Value Line's Median Appreciation Potential (MAP)
7. S&P 500's Reversion to the Mean

Refined January Barometer

The January Barometer was devised by Yale Hirsch, the long-time editor of *The Stock Trader's Almanac*. He first mentioned this indicator in 1972.

According to Hirsch's January Barometer, "As January goes, so goes the year." That is, a positive January for the S&P 500 forecasts a positive year as a whole for the Index, and a negative January forecasts a negative year as a whole. Personally, I don't like the fact that there is an overlap: January is part of the year as a whole. As a result, I **refined** the **January Barometer** to be January and the next 11 months of the year.

Barron's thought my refinement had merit, because they published my article, "January's Child," on Christmas Day, 2000. Although my refinement was logical, the results of the refined January Barometer left a lot to be desired. For example, immediately after the article was published, the S&P 500 gained 3.5% for January 2001, but lost 16.0% for the remaining 11 months of the year! For 2014, the S&P 500 lost 3.5% in January but gained 15.5% for the remaining 11 months of the year. For 2001–2015 (15 years), the refined January Barometer failed in seven years. And at this writing (August 31, 2016), 2016 is looking like a failure too.

TIAA Real Estate Fund

This Fund is one of the nine funds that are the core of the TIAA-CREF retirement program for employees of universities and some not-for-profit organizations. Table E-1 indicates the **TIAA Real Estate Fund** has had only one pullback greater than 1.34% from October 2, 1995 (its inception) to September 23, 2016 (the date this section was written).

Table E-1
TIAA Real Estate Fund, October 2, 1995 to September 23, 2016

These major moves are based on a criterion of a ±1.35% change in the Fund's price.

Turning Points		Gain or Loss	Trading Days
10/02/95	06/24/08	211.1%	3,204
06/24/08	03/11/10	−40.0%	431
03/11/10	09/23/16*	99.6%	1,647
*and counting			

I developed a successful market-timing model for the Fund. The model was launched in October 2004. So far, I have made only three trades:

Signal	Date	Price	Top or Bottom		Difference in price
Buy	10/15/04	$204.38			
Sell	08/04/08	$314.43	06/24/08	$314.98	$0.55
Buy	04/07/10	$190.00	03/11/10	$188.94	$1.06

I had a very large portion of my IRA portfolio invested in the Fund from 10/15/04 to 08/04/08, and from 04/07/10 to the present (09/23/16). I wish all my market-timing models had worked this well!

Value Line's Median Appreciation Potential (MAP)

The Value Line Investment Survey, published weekly, has a universe of about 1,700 stocks. For each of the stocks, Value Line forecasts its appreciation potential over the next three years. Then, the appreciation potential for each of the 1,700 stocks is ranked. The **MAP** is the appreciation potential for the median stock, the one ranked 850th.

Daniel A. Seiver is a main proponent of the MAP as a market-timing indicator. Seiver is editor of an investment newsletter, *PAD System Report*.[4]

---

4 "PAD" stands for patience and discipline. The *PAD System Report* is based on Seiver's book, *Outsmarting Wall Street* (McGrawHill, 1994).

Kip Karney and I purchased the MAP data going back to its origin in 1973 Despite a good college try, we found few useful relationships in the MAP data. As a result, we never completed a market-timing model based on the MAP data.

S&P 500's Reversion to the Mean

A short section in Chapter 1 discusses reversion to the mean (p. 12). In 2012, I started but never finished a book manuscript on the S&P 500's reversion to the mean. While working on this project, I wrote a short paper, "An Intriguing Forecasting Model," which appears below. I thought *Barron's* might publish this paper, but—after requesting and receiving my rewrite—they rejected it. I was disappointed.

Charles Long, a retired engineer and along-time reviewer of my writing (and one of my best reviewers), was disappointed too. He thought the paper delivered an interesting and informative message. You can decide if you agree with Charles.

"An Intriguing Forecasting Model"

John K. Harris, Ph.D.
Professor Emeritus of Accounting
University of Tulsa

Forecasting annual stock-market returns may not be folly, as some experts claim. There is a clue in history that suggests this forecast: A period of above-average returns for the S&P 500 to start in 2012 and continue for four years or more. The clue comes from mining the history of the S&P 500's annual returns with an eye to the powerful principle of reversion to the mean (RTM).

Many investors believe that forecasting the stock market is a fool's errand. The experts' message is unequivocal: Relying on stock market forecasts will be hazardous to the investor's wealth. Nonetheless, human nature drives the demand for and supply of stock market forecasts, and so forecasts abound.

Remarkably, twice in the 20th century, it would have been possible—guided by the high likelihood that the S&P 500's annual returns would revert to their long-term mean—to forecast periods of four years or more that, as a group, did have above-average S&P 500 returns. Now, a third such possibility is at hand.

RTM, is an immutable principle in financial markets borne out by history. According to this principle: (1) periods of above-average returns tend to occur after periods of below-average returns and (2) periods of above-average returns tend to be followed by periods of below-average returns. A manifestation of RTM is that annual returns over, say, any 25-year period tend to have an arithmetic average (mean) that is the same as or similar to their long-term mean.

The S&P 500's mean annual return for its [then] entire 86-year history, 1926–2011, is 12.8%. The returns for individual years varied widely, ranging from the highs of 54.0% for 1933 and 52.6% for 1954 to the lows of −43.3% for 1931 and −37.0% for 2008. To illustrate RTM for a few 25-year periods, the S&P 500's mean annual return was 10.9% for 1926–1950, 13.4% for 1937–1961, 12.8% for 1946–1970 and 12.5% for 1977–2011.

RTM can be the basis of a simple investment strategy. The investor would adjust his asset allocation based on two metrics driven by RTM: (1) the S&P 500's 15-year mean annual returns and (2) the S&P 500's returns for individual years. The trigger values for these metrics were determined by analyzing the history of the S&P 500's annual returns.

Trigger 1: *The S&P 500's 15-year mean annual return is ≤9.0% for any two consecutive years.* Historically, this particular mean annual return has been at a relatively low level sometimes. It occurred 13 times during 1940–2011, the 72-year period for which the S&P 500's 15-year mean annual return can be calculated. See Table 1. The occurrence rate was 18.1% (13 ÷ 72). This trigger signals the investor to depart from his normal asset allocation and overweight stocks (for our purposes, the S&P 500) and underweight bonds in his portfolio for the following year.

Trigger 2: *The S&P 500's 15-year mean annual return is ≥19.0% for any year.* Historically, this particular mean annual return has been at an extremely high level sometimes. It occurred only twice during the 72-year period—1956 and 1999— for an occurrence rate of 2.8%. See Table 1. This trigger signals the investor to underweight the S&P 500 and overweight bonds for the following year: 1957 and 2000, which had annual returns of −10.8% and −9.1%, respectively.

Table 1
Application of the RTM Forecasting Model's Trigger 1 and Trigger 2, 1940–2018

To compute 15-year mean annual returns for 2012–2018, returns for that period were assumed to be at a high level of 15.0% per year.

15 Years	15-Year S&P 500 Mean Annual Return	Final Year in 15-Year Period	S&P 500 Annual Return	Remarks
1926–40	8.5%	1940		
1927–41	7.0%	1941		
1928–42	5.8%	1942	20.3%	Trigger 1
1929–43	4.7%	1943	25.9%	Trigger 1
1930–44	6.5%	1944	19.8%	Trigger 1
1931–45	10.6%	1945	36.4%	Trigger 1
1932–46	13.0%	1946		
1933–47	13.9%	1947		
1934–48	10.7%	1948		
1935–49	12.0%	1949		
1936–50	11.0%	1950		
1937–51	10.3%	1951		
1938–52	13.9%	1952		
1939–53	11.7%	1953		
1940–54	15.2%	1954		
1941–55	18.0%	1955		
1942–56	19.2%	1956		
1943–57	17.1%	1957	−10.8%	Trigger 2
1944–58	18.3%	1958		
1945–59	17.8%	1959		
1946–60	15.4%	1960		
1947–61	17.7%	1961		
1948–62	16.8%	1962		
1949–63	17.9%	1963		
1950–64	17.8%	1964		
1951–65	16.5%	1965		
1952–66	14.2%	1966		
1953–67	14.6%	1967		
1954–68	15.4%	1968		
1955–69	11.3%	1969		
1956–70	9.5%	1970		
1957–71	10.0%	1971		

Table 1 (Continued)

15 Years	15-Year S&P 500 Mean Annual Return	Final Year in 15-Year Period	S&P 500 Annual Return	Remarks
1958–72	12.0%	1972		
1959–73	8.1%	1973		
1960–74	5.5%	1974		
1961–75	8.0%	1975	37.2%	Trigger 1
1962–76	7.8%	1976	23.8%	Trigger 1
1963–77	7.9%	1977	−7.2%	Trigger 1
1964–78	6.8%	1978	6.6%	Trigger 1
1965–79	6.9%	1979	18.4%	Trigger 1
1966–80	8.3%	1980	32.4%	Trigger 1
1967–81	8.6%	1981	−4.9%	Trigger 1
1968–82	8.4%	1982	21.4%	Trigger 1
1969–83	9.2%	1983	22.5%	Trigger 1
1970–84	10.2%	1984		
1971–85	12.1%	1985		
1972–86	12.3%	1986		
1973–87	11.4%	1987		
1974–88	13.5%	1988		
1975–89	17.4%	1989		
1976–90	14.7%	1990		
1977–91	15.1%	1991		
1978–92	16.1%	1992		
1979–93	16.4%	1993		
1980–94	15.2%	1994		
1981–95	15.5%	1995		
1982–96	17.4%	1996		
1983–97	18.2%	1997		
1984–98	18.6%	1998		
1985–99	19.6%	1999		
1986–00	16.8%	2000	−9.1%	Trigger 2
1987–01	14.8%	2001		
1988–02	13.0%	2002		
1989–03	13.8%	2003		
1990–04	12.4%	2004		
1991–05	13.0%	2005		
1992–06	12.0%	2006		

Table 1 (Continued)

15 Years	15-Year S&P 500 Mean Annual Return	Final Year in 15-Year Period	S&P 500 Annual Return	Remarks
1993–07	11.8%	2007		
1994–08	8.7%	2008		
1995–09	10.4%	2009		
1996–10	8.9%	2010		
1997–11	7.5%	2011		
1998–12	6.3%	2012	?	Trigger 1
1999–13	5.4%	2013	?	Trigger 1
2000–14	5.0%	2014	?	Trigger 1
2001–15	6.6%	2015	?	Trigger 1
2002–16	8.4%	2016	?	Trigger 1
2003–17	10.8%	2017	?	Trigger 1
2004–18	9.9%	2018		

Trigger 3: *The S&P 500's 15-year mean annual return minus the long-term government bonds 15-year mean annual return is ≤2.7% for any year.* Historically, this particular difference between the 15-year mean annual returns has been at a relatively low level sometimes. It occurred 14 times during the 72-year period, for an occurrence rate of 19.4%. See Table 2. This trigger signals the investor to overweight the S&P 500 and underweight bonds for the following year. The years already identified in Table 1 were 1942–45, 1975 and 1983. The additional years identified in Table 2 were 1985, 1988, 1996, 2003, 2006, 2009, 2010 and 2011. The S&P 500's mean annual return in the eight additional years was 20.0%.

Trigger 4: *The S&P 500's 15-year mean annual return minus the long-term government bonds 15-year mean annual return is ≥17.0% for any year.* Historically, this particular difference between the 15-year mean annual returns has been at an extremely high level sometimes. It occurred four times during the 72-year period, for an occurrence rate of 5.6%. See Table 2. This trigger signals the investor to underweight the S&P 500 and overweight bonds for the following year. The year already identified in Table 1 was 1957. The additional years identified were 1959, 1960 and 1962. The S&P 500's mean annual return in those three years was 1.3%.

Table 2
Application of the RTM Forecasting Model's Trigger 3 and Trigger 4, 1940-2011

LTGB = Long-Term Government Bonds

15 Years	15-Year S&P 500 Mean Annual Return	15-Year LTGB Mean Annual Return	15-Year Difference in Mean Annual Return	Final Year in 15-Year Period	S&P 500 Annual Return	Remarks
1926–40	8.5%	5.1%	3.4%	1940		
1927–41	7.0%	4.7%	2.3%	1941		
1928–42	5.8%	4.3%	1.6%	1942	20.3%	Trigger 3
1929–43	4.7%	4.4%	0.2%	1943	25.9%	Trigger 3
1930–44	6.5%	4.4%	2.2%	1944	19.8%	Trigger 3
1931–45	10.6%	4.8%	5.9%	1945	36.4%	Trigger 3
1932–46	13.0%	5.1%	7.9%	1946		
1933–47	13.9%	3.8%	10.1%	1947		
1934–48	10.7%	4.1%	6.6%	1948		
1935–49	12.0%	3.8%	8.2%	1949		
1936–50	11.0%	3.5%	7.5%	1950		
1937–51	10.3%	2.7%	7.6%	1951		
1938–52	13.9%	2.8%	11.1%	1952		
1939–53	11.7%	2.7%	9.1%	1953		
1940–54	15.2%	1.8%	13.5%	1954		
1941–55	18.0%	1.3%	16.7%	1955		
1942–56	19.2%	0.9%	18.4%	1956		
1943–57	17.1%	1.1%	16.0%	1957	−10.8%	Trigger 4
1944–58	18.3%	0.6%	17.7%	1958		
1945–59	17.8%	0.3%	17.5%	1959	12.0%	Trigger 4
1946–60	15.4%	0.5%	14.9%	1960	0.5%	Trigger 4
1947–61	17.7%	0.5%	17.2%	1961		
1948–62	16.8%	1.2%	15.6%	1962	−8.7%	Trigger 4
1949–63	17.9%	1.0%	16.9%	1963		
1950–64	17.8%	0.8%	16.9%	1964		
1951–65	16.5%	0.9%	15.6%	1965		
1952–66	14.2%	1.4%	12.8%	1966		
1953–67	14.6%	0.7%	13.9%	1967		
1954–68	15.4%	0.4%	15.0%	1968		
1955–69	11.3%	0.6%	10.7%	1969		
1956–70	9.5%	1.5%	8.0%	1970		

Table 2 (Continued)

15 Years	15-Year S&P 500 Mean Annual Return	15-Year LTGB Mean Annual Return	15-Year Difference in Mean Annual Return	Final Year in 15-Year Period	S&P 500 Annual Return	Remarks
1957–71	10.0%	2.7%	7.3%	1971		
1958–72	12.0%	2.6%	9.4%	1972		
1959–73	8.1%	2.9%	5.2%	1973		
1960–74	5.5%	3.4%	2.2%	1974		
1961–75	8.0%	3.1%	4.9%	1975	37.2%	Trigger 3
1962–76	7.8%	4.1%	3.7%	1976		
1963–77	7.9%	3.6%	4.3%	1977		
1964–78	6.8%	3.4%	3.4%	1978		
1965–79	6.9%	3.1%	3.8%	1979		
1966–80	8.3%	2.8%	5.4%	1980		
1967–81	8.6%	2.7%	5.9%	1981		
1968–82	8.4%	6.0%	2.4%	1982		
1969–83	9.2%	6.1%	3.1%	1983	22.5%	Trigger 3
1970–84	10.2%	7.4%	2.7%	1984		
1971–85	12.1%	8.7%	3.4%	1985	32.2%	Trigger 3
1972–86	12.3%	9.4%	2.9%	1986		
1973–87	11.4%	8.9%	2.5%	1987		
1974–88	13.5%	9.6%	3.9%	1988	16.8%	Trigger 3
1975–89	17.4%	10.5%	6.9%	1989		
1976–90	14.7%	10.3%	4.4%	1990		
1977–91	15.1%	10.5%	4.6%	1991		
1978–92	16.1%	11.1%	5.1%	1992		
1979–93	16.4%	12.4%	4.0%	1993		
1980–94	15.2%	11.9%	3.3%	1994		
1981–95	15.5%	14.3%	1.2%	1995		
1982–96	17.4%	14.1%	3.3%	1996	23.1%	Trigger 3
1983–97	18.2%	12.5%	5.7%	1997		
1984–98	18.6%	13.3%	5.3%	1998		
1985–99	19.6%	11.7%	7.9%	1999		
1986–00	16.8%	11.1%	5.8%	2000		
1987–01	14.8%	9.7%	5.2%	2001		
1988–02	13.0%	11.0%	2.0%	2002		
1989–03	13.8%	10.5%	3.3%	2003	28.7%	Trigger 3
1990–04	12.4%	9.8%	2.6%	2004		

Table 2 (Continued)

15 Years	15-Year S&P 500 Mean Annual Return	15-Year LTGB Mean Annual Return	15-Year Difference in Mean Annual Return	Final Year in 15-Year Period	S&P 500 Annual Return	Remarks
1991–05	13.0%	10.0%	3.0%	2005	4.9%	Trigger 3
1992–06	12.0%	8.7%	3.2%	2006		
1993–07	11.8%	8.9%	3.0%	2007		
1994–08	8.7%	9.4%	−0.7%	2008		
1995–09	10.4%	10.9%	−0.5%	2009	26.5%	Trigger 3
1996–10	8.9%	9.5%	−0.6%	2010	15.1%	Trigger 3
1997–11	7.5%	11.4%	−3.9%	2011	2.1%	Trigger 3

Of course, these triggers were developed by data mining. Although data mining is the common criticism of stock market forecasting models, the immutable principle of RTM suggests that criticism would have little or no validity for the RTM forecasting model—unless a sizable change occurs in the S&P 500's long-term mean annual return and/or a decrease occurs in the volatility of individual years.

For simplicity in the examples that follow, assume the investor uses two asset classes, the S&P 500 and long-term government bonds. For all the years that the RTM forecasting model did not over-weight or under-weight the S&P 500, the investor using the model would maintain his normal asset allocation. Because of the extremes represented in the four triggers, it is safe to say that market risk would not have been higher for the years in which the S&P 500 was over-weighted or under-weighted compared to the overall level of risk for all normal-weighted years during 1940–2011.

Based on the RTM forecasting model, the 13 years identified in Table 1 occurred in two clusters, four years and nine years, respectively. Will 2012's over-weighting signal continue for a cluster of years? If so, how long will the cluster last? Nobody knows, of course, but stock market history suggests some possibilities. Even if the mean annual return for 2012–2014 were a very high 30%, for example, the 15-year mean annual return going into the next year (2015) would be 8.0%—signaling yet another year of above-mean performance. And the same kind of analysis suggests that 2016, and even additional years, could be included in this new cluster.

Table 3 is a recap of the RTM forecasting model's signals. There were 21 signals to over-weight the S&P 500 and five signals to under-weight it during 1940–2011.

The year 2012 also is a year to over-weight the S&P 500. Only five of the 26 signals (19%) were incorrect. Although the S&P 500's return was only 6.6% for 1978 (about half of the long-term mean), that over-weight signal can be judged to be correct because all types of bonds had returns of less than 6.6% for 1978.

Table 3
Over-Weight or Under-Weight the
S&P 500, 1940–2011

The dividing line separates 1940–2011 into two periods of 36 years.

Year	S&P 500 Weighting	Trigger	S&P 500 Return	Was the Weighting Decision Correct?
1942	Over	1 & 3	20.3%	Yes
1943	Over	1 & 3	25.9%	Yes
1944	Over	1 & 3	19.8%	Yes
1945	Over	1 & 3	36.4%	Yes
1957	Under	2 & 4	−10.8%	Yes
1959	Under	4	12.0%	No
1960	Under	4	0.5%	Yes
1962	Under	4	−8.7%	Yes
1975	Over	1 & 3	37.2%	Yes
1976	Over	1	23.8%	Yes
1977	Over	1	−7.2%	No
1978	Over	1	6.6%	Yes
1979	Over	1	18.4%	Yes
1980	Over	1	32.4%	Yes
1981	Over	1	−4.9%	No
1982	Over	1	21.4%	Yes
1983	Over	1 & 3	22.5%	Yes
1985	Over	3	32.2%	Yes
1988	Over	3	16.8%	Yes
1996	Over	3	23.1%	Yes
2000	Under	2	−9.1%	Yes
2003	Over	3	28.7%	Yes
2005	Over	3	4.9%	No
2009	Over	3	26.5%	Yes
2010	Over	3	15.1%	Yes
2011	Over	3	2.1%	No
2012	Over	1	?	?

Implementing the RTM forecasting model's over-weight signals for the S&P 500 would have been simple. Just modestly increase the investor's asset allocation to the S&P 500 for those years; in today's stock market, that could be done with the exchange-traded fund, stock symbol SPY. Conversely, modestly decrease the allocation for under-weight signals for those years. If the modest increases and decreases are thought to have a rational basis, then that strategy is called tactical asset allocation (TAA).[5]

John Bogle observed: "Sometimes, the manifestation of RTM requires patience!"[6] The wisdom of this statement is evidenced by the fact that the normal asset allocation for the TAA investor was in effect for 56 of the 72 years during 1940–2011. The normal-allocation prevailed for three long spans in Table 3: 11 years (1946–1956), 17 years (1958–1974) and 16 years (1984–1999). For 1940–2011, the RTM forecasting model identified 22 years to over-weight the S&P 500 and five years to under-weight it. On average, the TAA investor made annual departures from his normal asset allocation only once ever 4.5 years.

Will the RTM forecast now in force be folly? Time will tell. However, history suggests that the 15-year mean annual return at the end of 2011 is pointing to a cluster of four or more years of above-average S&P 500 returns. It will be interesting to find out if this forecasted cluster is a case that rewards investors for having the patience to allow the S&P 500's RTM to manifest itself.[7]

In conclusion, here are two strong, perhaps unique, points about the RTM forecasting model versus all other models to forecast the stock market: (1) Data mining is unlikely to be a problem and (2) The RTM anomaly is unlikely to disappear in the years to come.

---

5   John C. Bogle, *Common Sense on Mutual Funds* (Wiley 1999), p. 66.

6   John C. Bogle, *Common Sense on Mutual Funds* (Wiley 1999), p. 228.

7   The four-year cluster (2012–2015) did indeed reward S&P 500 investors: That mean annual return was 16% compared to the 1966–2015 mean annual return of 11%. For the year 2016, the S&P 500 return was 12.5%; as I go to press on 11/26/17, the S&P 500 year-to-date is 18.4%. So, my RTM model has generated outstanding results for the 2012–2017 cluster of years!

Appendix F

◇◇◇◇◇◇◇◇◇◇◇◇◇

Investing in Good Times and Bad Times[1]

The S&P 500, a widely-used measure of the U.S. stock market, moves in major cycles that are comprised of "good times" and "bad times." These cycles were prominent during 1995–2014:

Period	S&P 500 Change	Years	Major Cycle
Jan 3, 1995 – Mar 24, 2000	233%	5.2	#1 Good times
Mar 24, 2000 – Oct 9, 2002	−49%	2.6	#1 Bad times
Oct 9, 2002 – Oct 9, 2007	101%	5.0	#2 Good times
Oct 9, 2007 – Mar 9, 2009	−57%	1.4	#2 Bad times
Mar 9, 2009 – Dec 31, 2014	204%	5.8	#3 Good times

As with most other major cycles in the S&P 500's [then] 87-year history, there is a sharp contrast between gains in good times and losses in bad times, and good times last considerably longer than bad times. As of December 31, 2014, bad times have not yet begun.

Continued on next page.

---

1 This strategy was put in the "trash can of failed strategies" in March 2016.

Consider the brand new proprietary investment strategy:
Good and Bad Times (GBT) Model
The GBT model was completed at the end of 2014. Its back-testing started at the beginning of 1928, the origin of the S&P 500's daily prices. The model, which can be used by any investor for a small or large portion of his portfolio, had remarkable performance for 1928–2014—mainly because it signaled (1) to be invested in the S&P 500 during much of its good times and (2) not to be invested there during much of its bad times.
If interested, read on!

In an objective and systematic way, the GBT model's purpose is to follow Warren Buffett's sage investment advice: "Be fearful when others are greedy and greedy when others are fearful." His advice aligns with the fact that greed and fear drive the financial markets (the S&P 500 for our purposes). In a major market cycle, greed is the prevailing sentiment at the top, and fear is the prevailing sentiment at the bottom. The cycle turns down when greed begins to lessen (that is, the buyers become exhausted), and the cycle turns up when fear begins to lessen (that is, the sellers become exhausted).

The extremes reached by greed and fear in the S&P 500's major cycles are controlled by a strong force. This force—called reversion to the mean—operates like a powerful magnet pulling the S&P 500's performance down after periods of above-average performance, and pulling its performance up after periods of below-average performance. As a result, the S&P 500's returns over, say, almost any 20-year period tend to have an arithmetic average (a mean) that is nearly the same as their long-term mean. The S&P 500's mean annual return for 1928–2014 was 11.8%.

For good times, the GBT model identifies a day thought to be an opportune time to buy the S&P 500—a Buy signal. For bad times, the model identifies a day thought to be an opportune time to sell the S&P 500—a Sell signal. Buy and sell signals alternate. For the S&P 500's entire history, 1928–2014, there have been 22 Sell signals and 22 Buy signals. A Sell signal occurred on average about once every four years, but several of those signals were less than 90 days apart. Sixty-four percent of the Sell signals were in effect at the time of bear market lows.

A simple way to think about the GBT model is by means of an imaginary traffic signal that has two colors: green and red. This signal changes to green when a signal to buy the S&P 500 occurs and changes to red when a signal to sell the S&P 500 occurs. For 1928–2014, the traffic signal was green 83% of the time and red 17%.

When this writeup was completed (March 10, 2015), the GBT model's two most recent signals were to sell December 18, 2007 (S&P 500 1454.98) and to buy May 19, 2009 (S&P 500 908.13). The next signal—whenever it occurs—will be to sell.

Note 1: Past performance of the GBT model is no guarantee of future results.

Note 2: The S&P 500 is a market-value weighted index of 500 of the largest U.S. companies. The S&P 500, which comprised about 78% of the total value of the U.S. stock market at the end of 2014, has included 500 companies since March 4, 1957. Prior to that date and going back to its origin at the beginning of 1928, the Index included 90 large companies. In this writeup, "S&P 500" will be used for the entire period since 1928.

Who Can Use the GBT Model?

◆ Individual investors having an employer-sponsored retirement plan [401(k), 403(b), 457 or Thrift Savings Plan] a Traditional IRA, a SEP IRA or a Roth IRA.

◆ Individual investors having taxable accounts. (Of course, trades in these accounts are subject to income taxes that diminish returns, depending on the investor's particular circumstances.)

◆ Institutional investors: pension funds, endowments and foundations.

The Model's Past Performance

The GBT model was developed for 1940–2014, and then back-tested for 1928–1939. The performance for 1928–1939 was far better than the good performance for 1940–2014. After that successful test of the model, the two periods were combined for purposes of the following insightful comparisons to buying-and-holding the S&P 500.

If $1,000 had been invested in the S&P 500 at the beginning of 1928 and held until the end of 2014, the total accumulation (including reinvested dividends) would have been nearly $3.5 million. Assuming that the $1,000 had been managed using the GBT model for 1928–2014, the total accumulation (including reinvested dividends and interest) would have been a mind-boggling $53.2 million. *That's 14 times more!* (For simplicity, these GBT calculations used an annual interest rate of 3% for the time not invested in the S&P 500—the time from each Sell signal to the following Buy signal.)

The main reason for the $49.7 million difference between the total accumulations is that the GBT model greatly limited downside risk compared to buying-and-holding the S&P 500. For 1928–2014, some three-fourths of the *sell-to-buy trades* were winners (that is, the S&P 500 was sold and then later repurchased at a lower price). These trades had an average gain of 14.5%. For the other sell-to-buy trades, the average was −3.6%. Only one sell-to-buy trade had a loss exceeding 4%: −6.8% in 1937. Only one sequence of three consecutive sell-to-buy trades had a loss greater than 1%: −6.4% during 1990–1994.

For 1982–2014 (33 years), the S&P 500 had a negative annual return five times, averaging 16.6%. In contrast, the GBT model had a negative annual return four times; the largest was only 3.2%.

Be aware that these measures of downside risk do not mean the GBT model is a low-risk strategy. For example, the model had a Buy signal in effect during both the Crash of 1929 and the Crash of 1987; for those terrifying times, the S&P 500's maximum declines were 44.7% and 33.2%, respectively—the largest and 4th largest in its history when the traffic signal was green. A recent example: The S&P 500 declined 19.4% from late April to early October of 2011 and the traffic signal was green throughout that year. *For 1928–2014, it is obvious that using the GBT model would have involved substantial risk but much less risk than buying-and-holding the S&P 500.*

The following comparisons clearly indicate the outstanding performance of the GBT model for the last 20 years:

Time Period	Mean Annual Return		GBT Advantage
	GBT	S&P 500	
5 Years			
1995–1999	28.7%	28.7%	—-
2000–2004	7.3%	−0.7%	8.0%
2005–2009	10.7%	3.1%	7.6%
2010–2014	15.9%	15.9%	—-
The two years GBT outperformed the S&P 500 by the most since 2000			
2002	−3.4%	−22.1%	18.7%
2008	1.5%	−37.0%	38.5%
The only year GBT underperformed the S&P 500 since 2000			
2009	25.8%	26.5%	−0.7%

The bottom line for 1928–2014 is that, compared to buying-and-holding the S&P 500, the GBT model achieved much higher mean annual returns while taking much lower risk. In contrast, conventional investing wisdom says that, over long time periods, achieving higher mean annual returns can only be accomplished by taking higher risk.

Sleeping Well in the Worst of the Bad Times

It is painful for investors to see their portfolios plummet during major declines in the S&P 500. By design, a spectacular feature of the GBT model has often come into play in those times: The traffic signal was red during much of the time that the S&P 500 had extended periods of its worst performance. For five of the worst times in S&P 500 history—1930–1932, 1937, 1973–1974, 2000–02 and 2008—the S&P 500 had a mean annual return of –23.3%. The GBT model's mean annual return for those 10 years was –3.0%. As a result, the GBT investor would have been spared much anxiety.

Using or Monitoring the Model

The GBT model's future signals will be sent in real time "To Those Interested." The signals are being made available now free of charge to show you the real-time performance of the model as the future unfolds.[2] You have two options:

1. Use the model for a small or large portion of your portfolio. You will receive three types of email:
   - ◆ Brief S&P 500 updates a week or so after the end of each calendar quarter.
   - ◆ Alerts when a Buy or Sell signal is likely to occur during the next several trading days.
   - ◆ Alerts when a Buy or Sell signal will occur that day if a specific level of the S&P 500 is reached at the market close. These alerts will be sent at about 1:00 pm Eastern time—that's three hours before the market closes—to allow you time to execute the trade.

2. Monitor the model as the future unfolds. You will receive the same emails as above.

   Whether you use or monitor, keep in mind: For 1928–2014, the S&P 500 moved in major cycles, and the GBT model took advantage of that fact to decisively outperform buying-and-holding the S&P 500. The S&P 500 undoubtedly will continue to move in major cycles. Of course, time will tell if the model outperforms in the future.

---

2   As of November 2017, that email distribution has been replaced by the G&P free email distribution (p. 131).

How To Use the Model

There are two approaches: have a brokerage account or not have a brokerage account.

Brokerage Account. The preferred approach is for the GBT investor to have a brokerage account and trade exchange-traded funds (ETFs) as follows:

a. At the market close the day the traffic signal changes from green to red:

- ◆ Sell the S&P 500 index fund (stock symbol SPY).
- ◆ Use the proceeds from that trade to buy Treasury bills [or the Vanguard Short-Term Bond Index Fund (BSV)[3]] or—if taking higher risk is desired—to buy the ProShares Short S&P 500 (SH). This trade aims to generate a positive return while the traffic signal is red.

b. At the market close the day the traffic signal changes from red to green:

- ◆ Sell Treasury bills, BSV or SH.
- ◆ Use the proceeds from that trade to buy SPY.

Of course, to get started using the GBT model, the GBT investor's portfolio should include SPY if the signal is green or Treasury bills, BSV or SH if the traffic signal is red.

Using ETFs, the online trading cost of each trade is typically under $10, regardless of the dollar amount of the trade. The total fees charged by ETFs recommended for the GBT investor are extremely low, except for SH.

No Brokerage Account. If the GBT investor doesn't have a brokerage account [for example, she has a 401(k)], trades ideally would involve index mutual funds that charge fees of no more than 0.25% per year. Otherwise, use the lowest-cost (lowest expense-ratio) funds available. The trades are as follows:

a. At the market close the day the traffic signal turns red:

- ◆ Sell a large-company stock mutual fund.
- ◆ Use the proceeds from that trade to buy a bond mutual fund (short term is preferable to longer term) or put the proceeds in a money market fund. This trade aims to generate a positive return while the traffic signal is red.

b. At the market close the day the traffic signal turns green:

- ◆ Sell the bond mutual fund or money market fund.
- ◆ Use the proceeds from that trade to buy a large-company stock mutual fund.

---

3   On 11/22/17, BSV's SEC yield was 1.90%. On the same date, the SEC yield on Vanguard's several money market funds ranged from 1.05% to 1.17%.

To get started, the GBT investor's portfolio should include a large-company fund if the traffic signal is green or a short-term bond fund or money market fund if the signal is red. In the case of an employer-sponsored retirement plan, regular monthly contributions should be put into the same fund held based on the signal being green or red.

Note 1: When deciding whether to invest in an ETF or a mutual fund, always read the current prospectus before investing.

Note 2: To discourage market timing, many mutual fund companies charge a redemption fee (often 1%) when the investor sells one of their funds not held for, say, at least 90 days. In those situations, the redemption fees for the GBT trades over the long term would have been minimal in the context of the model's outstanding performance.

Note 3: To keep investment fees as low as possible, the GBT investor should choose ETFs or index mutual funds instead of actively-managed mutual funds. That's because *some 61% of all actively-managed, large-company stock funds underperformed the S&P 500 over the past 25 years.* That underperformance was largely due to their high management fees and trading costs. As a result the investor who buys actively-managed funds must be feeling lucky!

Note 4: It is not desirable to use the GBT model for individual stocks, because they are much more volatile than ETFs or mutual funds.

Discipline and Patience

While the model had outstanding, back-tested performance for 1928–2014, be aware that the GBT investor would have needed to control his emotions to attain that performance—a challenge that is much easier said than done. To control emotions, discipline and patience are required. Intellect is the basis for both discipline and patience.

References for Appendix F

Bernstein, Peter L., *Against the Gods: The Remarkable Story of Risk* (Wiley, 1998).

Bogle, John C., *Common Sense on Mutual Funds: New Imperatives for the Intelligent Investor* (Wiley, 1999).

Housel, Morgan, "Don't Fear the Bear Market," *The Wall Street Journal* (February 14–15, 2015), p. B8.

Hulbert, Mark, "One Way to Time the Market," *The Wall Street Journal* (April 19, 2013).

Ibbotson SBBI 2015 Classic Yearbook: Market Results for Stocks, Bonds, Bills and Inflation (Morningstar).

Jakab, Spencer, "Yes, You Can Time the Market," *The Wall Street Journal* (August 22, 2014), p. C1.

Lorie, James H. and Mary T. Hamilton, *The Stock Market: Theories and Evidence* (Irwin, 1973).

McCulley, Paul, "The Shadow Banking System and Hyman Minsky's Economic Journey," *Insights Into the Global Financial Crisis*, Research Foundation of CFA Institute (December 2009).

Minsky, Hyman P., *Stabilizing An Unstable Economy* (McGraw-Hill, 2008).

Minsky, Hyman P., "The Financial Instability Hypothesis," The Levy Economics Institute of Bard College, Working Paper No. 74 (May 1992).

Shiller, Robert J., *Irrational Exuberance* (Princeton University Press, 2000).

Smithers, Andrew, *Wall Street Revalued: Imperfect Markets and Inept Central Bankers* (Wiley, 2009).

Smithers, Andrew and Stephen Wright, *Valuing Wall Street: Protecting Wealth in Turbulent Markets* (McGraw-Hill, 2000).

Taleb, Nassim Nicholas, *Fooled by Randomness: The Hidden Role of Chance in Life and in the Markets* (Random House Trade Paperbacks, 2005).

Appendix G

◇◇◇◇◇◇◇◇◇◇◇◇◇

Six Items From November 2017

This book was first published in October 2016. Few copies of it were sold prior to November 2017. I began actively promoting the book at that time based on refinements Kip Karney (my research partner) and I made in the grow-and-protect (G&P) model discussed in Chapters 3 and 4 (pp. 33–48). The refinements, which were completed in early Fall 2017, are the main reason this **"Revised First Edition"** was published in November 2017. *Kip Karney's and my research is on-going.*

A spike in book sales occurred in November 2017. This pleasant development made it necessary to write the G&P Orientation document and distribute it via email on 11/11/17; the document is presented below. *Very important: The material in this appendix incorporates the refinements in the G&P model (in its form as of 11/26/17).*

The newly-refined G&P model gave a half Sell signal at the opening of the stock market on 11/13/17. My email (#1 for 2017) telling of this signal is presented below. Next on 11/15/17, my email (#2 for 2017) telling of the other half Sell signal is presented below. Next, on 11/21/17, my email (#3 for 2017) telling of a full Buy signal is presented below. Then on 11/28/17, I emailed (#4 for 2017) announcing the Revised First Edition.

Finally, an email I received on 11/10/17 from a friend, whose wife is a retired minister of music, concludes this Appendix.

1. The G&P Orientation[1]

Thishis email list has grown significantly in recent weeks. I know most, but by no means all, of you personally. The purpose of this orientation is to get everyone "in the know" and "on the same page" regarding the nature of my future emails. If I materially revise this 11/26/17 version of the G&P orientation, I'll email you the new one. To be added to the free distribution list, email me:

harrisjohnk@hotmail.com

By way of introduction, I am a happily retired accounting professor who fishes a lot and enjoys tending a vegetable garden with my wife. My field of specialization was cost accounting in my academic career. Over my 30-year career, I did a lot of writing in that field. Since retiring at the end of 1996, my focus has changed to research and writing about the stock market. In today's world, the stock market is of interest to millions of investors because they have some of their financial wealth at stake there. Yet, many investors (with good intentions) actually know little about the stock market. That's the gap I hope to partially fill with this book and my emails.

In 1991, I received a coveted Outstanding Teacher Award at the University of Tulsa. Even at my age now (76), I still possess that skill set, which I used in writing this book and intend to use in the emails I'll send in the future. I'm engaging in this activity for as long as I'm able to do it.

In years when the stock market is doing well, I'll probably send about 6 to 8 emails. In years when the stock market is experiencing sizable downside moves, my emails will be more numerous. My first email at the beginning of each new calendar year will report on the performance of buying-and-holding the S&P 500 vs. the G&P model for the year just ended.

If you're on my distribution list, you can **unsubscribe** at any time upon request. Feel free to refer anyone to me to be added to the list; just have them email me that request: harrisjohnk@hotmail.com If you're so moved, tell your **Facebook friends** about this book and the related emails. As far as I'm concerned, the more the merrier!

Part Three of this book (pp. 59–78) reveals I'm a Christian and describes my spiritual journey, starting in 1957 (p. 62); I was 15 then. That journey, along with my life-long interest in investing and teaching, led me to write this book. Part Three will appeal to some readers but not others. In any case, that material

---

1   This item was originally sent to my email distribution list in mid-November 2017. As I go to press on this Revised First Edition, this is the 11/28/17 version of the G&P Orientation.

should **not** be interpreted as "God has shown me how to make accurate stock market forecasts."

Estimates are that investors collectively spend around **$100 billion a year** to manage their stock market investments (for example, the S&P 500). In sharp contrast, my email distributions are and always will be **free** to anyone who wants to receive them. Why? Because the Bible says being saved (that is, becoming a Christian) carries with it the promise of eternal life—which is a free gift from God to those who accept it.

Most of you are **individual investors**. Your knowledge of the stock market ranges from extensive to limited. You probably have a moderate or sizable portfolio in the form of a 401(k), 403(b), IRA and/or taxable account. I hope my emails also are of interest to **institutional investors** and **financial journalists**.

Because I am a teacher, my emails will frequently refer to specific pages in the G&P book (as I've done above). In Part One (pp. 1–31), you will learn a lot about the S&P 500—the sole object of my research—and today's conventional investing wisdom. In Part Two (pp. 33–57), you will see that I strongly disagree with today's conventional wisdom. As the future unfolds, I will challenge conventional wisdom with the G&P model. It's a classic David vs. Goliath confrontation, and the outcome is unknown at this time. Maybe in 10 years or so, the winner will be clear. Obviously, I expect that the G&P model will win!

It is important for you to understand the dual purposes of my emails:

(1) to document the G&P model's Buy and Sell signals in real time—that is, an on-going live test of the model—and

(2) to call your attention to the S&P 500's historical price movements that I deem relevant for education purposes and my own investment decisions.

These emails should not be construed as investment advice! Of course, some recipients could make investment decisions based on the emails, but that is **not** my intent.

The S&P Composite Index was launched at the beginning of 1928, some 90 years ago. Then it consisted of 90 stocks. It was expanded to 500 stocks in 1957. The historical movements in this Index fascinate and often befuddle investors.

I often refer to myself as a **stock market historian**. That's because I have published two books—*The Wall Street Traffic Light* (2008, out of print) and *The G&P Investment Strategy* (2016)—and my research has been cited in *Barron's* on numerous occasions (see p. 110).

Kip Karney, my research partner (a microbiologist), and I studied the historical movements of the S&P 500 in depth in relation to other variables to develop the G&P model. (Ironically, neither Kip nor I has taken a college investments course!) *Since the G&P book was originally published in October 2016, Kip and I have refined the G&P model. This process is on-going.* One important change in the latest version of the model is half **Buy** signals and half **Sell** signals. Usually, but not always, those signals are followed soon after by the other half of the **Buy** and **Sell** signals. To illustrate, suppose my total portfolio is in an IRA, consisting of 60% in stocks. If a half **Sell** signal occurs, I would change my portfolio to 30% stocks, putting the proceeds from the sale in a money market fund for safety. Then, if the other half of the **Sell** signal occurs, say, six trading days later, I would change my portfolio to 0% stocks, and put the proceeds from the selling of the other 30% of stocks in a money market fund. The net result of the two transactions is to completely move out of stocks and put the proceeds in a money market fund. Note: There are *no tax consequences* in this type of trade in IRAs, 401(k)s and 403(b)s—but **my role is not to give tax advice**.

The complete list of the 227 **G&P** trades for the 1966–2015 period—*before the G&P model was refined*—is in Table D-1 (pp. 96–102). Of those trades, 83 (36.6%) were unprofitable.

The **G&P** model is proprietary. That's because, if the model's formulas became widely known, it would perform poorly; see "Keeping a Secret," p. 50–51. But I offer this simple explanation of the **G&P** model's fundamental basis. In a unique and moderately-complex way, the model measures *investors' demand for and supply of S&P 500 stocks.* Historically, when demand exceeds supply, the S&P 500 will rise and the **G&P** model has tended to be on a **Buy** signal; historically, when supply exceeds demand, the S&P 500 will fall and the **G&P** model has tended to be on a **Sell** signal. This is the essence of what you need to know about the **G&P** model.

Bull market tops occur when buyers (the demand for S&P 500 stocks) become exhausted. Conversely, bear market bottoms occur when sellers (the supply of S&P 500 stocks) become exhausted.

I encourage you to email me your questions or comments about this orientation or my future emails. I'll try to respond within two or three days.

Regards,

John

2. Half Sell Signal at the 11/13/17 Market Open

From: John K. Harris
Sent: Sunday, November 12, 2017 (to my email distribution list)
Subject: Half Sell Signal at the 11/13/17 Market Open

Email #1 for 2017

> If you're so moved, forward this free email to anyone you wish. As far as I'm concerned, the more eyeballs that see it, the better. If you want to unsubscribe from my email distributions, please inform me.

Under the present circumstances, this email will be longer than most of my future emails.

The G&P Orientation explains that, based on on-going research regarding the G&P model (since the original publication of the G&P book in October 2016), half Buy and half Sell signals as well as full Buy and full Sell signals can occur. Using history as a guide, it's common for a half signal to become a full signal within, say, 1 to 15 more trading days.

In today's case, the half Sell signal will occur at tomorrow's market open. For purposes of calculating the G&P model's performance, I'll use the S&P 500's opening price. [The S&P 500 (S&P) closed on 11/10/17 at 2582.30.]

As of now, the S&P's all-time closing high was on 11/08/17 at 2594.38, just a smidgen shy of 2600.

Wall Street's criterion for a bear market is a decline of 20%. For example, if the S&P were to have a bear market from the 11/08/17 all-time high, it would need to fall to 2075.50 [2594.38 x (1.00 – 0.20)]. In Kip Karney's (my research partner) and my stock market research, we use a decline of 19% to denote a bear market. That's because there have been many cases when an S&P decline has been between 19.0% and 19.9%. That is, we find 19.0% to be a more useful criterion for a bear market for the purpose of analysis.

Using the 19.0% definition, here's a recap of the S&P's bull and bear market movements dating from the "once-in-a-generation" bear market low on 03/09/09:

Date	S&P 500	Change
03/09/09	676.53	
04/29/11	1363.61	+101.6%
10/03/11	1099.23	−19.4%
11/08/17	2594.38	+136.0%

You need to be aware of how dangerously high the S&P is now. So, look at the top of p. 108. As stated immediately before that tabulation, it was prepared on 07/31/16. As a result, the tabulation needs updating. From 07/31/16 to the S&P's all-time high on 11/08/17, Professor Shiller's CAPE rose 4.46 points, to 31.62. With that significant rise in mind, the updated tabulation is as follows:

	Number of Months	Bull Market Top
1929	1	09/07/29
7/1997–3/2000	33	03/24/00
	34	

That is, there were only 34 months in the history of the CAPE, which dates from January 1881 (nearly 137 years ago!), in which the CAPE was higher than it is now. From that starting date through October 2017, there were 1,642 months. Therefore, only **2.07%** of the months (34/1,642) had a higher CAPE than now. Obviously, now is an ideal time for the **G&P** model to speak its mind with a half **Sell** signal.

The Dos Equis XX beer commercials on TV always end by saying "Stay thirsty, my friends." Based on the 2.07% figure, I say **"Be very, very, very cautious, my fellow investors."**

Be alert to the possibility of the other half **Sell** signal occurring during the next couple of weeks. Of course, I'll send an email if and when that signal occurs.

Regards,

John

3. Other Half Sell Signal Today (11/15/17)

From: John K. Harris
Sent: Wednesday, November 15, 2017 (to my email distribution list)
Subject: Other Half Sell Signal Today (11/15/17)

Email #2 for 2017

> If you're so moved, forward this free email to anyone you wish. As far as I'm concerned, the more eyeballs that see it, the better. If you want to unsubscribe from my email distributions, please inform me.

An item that's relevant for you to keep handy is the G&P **Orientation document.** I emailed the first version to you on 11/11/17. The 11/26/17 version is on pp. 132–134.

As was the case with Email #1 for 2017, today's email will be much longer than the short ones I will normally send in the future. I know many of you are very busy people!

The other half Sell signal is today, 11/15/17. To be able to measure the G&P model's performance, I'll use today's closing S&P 500 (S&P). However, since I own an exchange-traded fund (ETF) in the remaining stock portion of my own portfolio, I'll sell the ETF sometime during the trading day.

A common view among many, many investors and most professional money managers is: **"Trying to guess the top (or bottom) of the S&P's movements using whatever type of indicator(s) is a fool's errand."** In fact, that statement is the essence of one of the tenets of modern portfolio theory (MPT) as currently taught at **every** business school in the US and around the world. See my book, Chapter 2, pp. 21–31.

MPT, which is today's conventional investing wisdom, leads to the conclusion that "what is important is the investor's time in the market, not his/her timing the market." In Chapter 3 of my book (pp. 35–43), I challenge MPT. That is, the G&P model was developed by Kip Karney (my research partner) and me for the purpose of market timing. So, this email is the latest in what will be a series of emails (announcing Buy and Sell signals) that will challenge MPT. In this head-to-head competition, time will tell whether the G&P model (David) or MPT (Goliath) will win.

The G&P model is 100% based on the S&P's history, which begins at the start of 1928. Back-testing was used to develop the G&P model. **MPT strongly disapproves of back-testing. I disagree. I contend that history is the best guide available to use for market timing (see my book, pp. 12–13).**

In my opinion, here's some relevant history that is interesting to consider today (11/15/17). Five cases in its history (with the sixth case being November 2017, not yet completed), **the S&P has had a winning streak of 300 or more trading days without a 5% pullback**. When you stop to think about it, these six cases are remarkable! My research on S&P winning streaks of various lengths without a 5% pullback has been cited in *Barron's* (see p. 110: #1 and #10). The six streaks of 300 or more trading days (td) are:

Case	Streak Ended	td	Subsequent Decline	
1	01/03/55	326	−5.90%	10 td
2	08/03/59	448	−9.17%	35 td
3	05/13/65	369	−9.60%	31 td
4	02/02/94	333	−8.94%	41 td
5	05/24/96	369	−7.63%	41 td
6	11/08/17?	440	?	?

While this table has nothing to do with the **G&P** model *per se*, the data are interesting nonetheless, especially right now.

By the way, the S&P tends to go up much more slowly than it goes down. In sharp contrast to the six **long winning streaks**, the S&P fell 20.47% on **a single day** (10/19/87), the Greatest Crash of all-time. Stunning! **And I can imagine that something similar could take place some day in the future, even in the near future.**

Interestingly, none of the first five cases was a bull market top. It is said, and I agree, that bull market tops occur when buyers (the demand for S&P stocks) become exhausted. Time will tell if 11/08/17 was a bull market top. If so, it was caused by buyer exhaustion. [Conversely, bear market bottoms occur when sellers (the supply of **G&P** stocks) become exhausted. The two most recent bear market lows by my reckoning are 03/09/09 and 04/29/11.]

I hope you have learned worthwhile things from this email. And **please remember,** as it says in the **G&P** Orientation, **this email should not be considered as investment advice**. I realize some recipients could make investment decisions based on the email, but that is **not** my intent.

Note that I will act on all signals in my own portfolio, which is an IRA—so, there are no tax consequences from trading.

Most of my future emails will be much shorter than this one. I promise.

Regards,

John

4. Full Buy Signal at Market Open 11/22/17

From: John K. Harris
Sent: Tuesday, November 21, 2017 (to my email distribution list)
Subject: Full Buy Signal at Market Open 11/22/17

Email #3 for 2017

> If you're so moved, forward this free email to anyone you wish. As far as I'm concerned, the more eyeballs that see it, the better. If you want to unsubscribe from my email distributions, please inform me.

The S&P 500 closed today at 2599.03, an all-time high. Obviously, that gives us a clear message that the demand for S&P stocks is exceeding the supply of S&P stocks. That situation can go on for a short or long period. So, I'm issuing a full Buy signal at tomorrow's open.

The average of the two half Sell signals last week is 2570.58. Assuming tomorrow's open happened to be equal to today's close (2599.03), the loss would be a mere 1.12% from being out of the S&P. The 1.12% is an example of wealth-self insurance [pp. 36, 40–41 column (6) and p. 43].

I'll be interested to see if this full Buy signal is a winner. Time will tell.

Happy Thanksgiving!

John

The three emails above certainly could lead to the wrong conclusion. That is, because the three signals occurred within a few days of each other, it appears that the G&P model is a fast-trading vehicle. Nothing could be further from the truth. The truth is revealed by looking at the bottom line in Table 3-2, column (2), p. 41; the mean number of trades per year for 1966–2015 was 4.6. In some years, the trades were close together timewise, as has happened in November 2017.

5. Announcing the Revised First Edition of My G&P Book

From: John K. Harris
Sent: Tuesday, November 28, 2017 (to my email distribution list)
Subject: Announcing the Revised First Edition of My G&P Book

Email #4 for 2017

> If you're so moved, forward this free email to anyone you wish. As far as I'm concerned, the more eyeballs that see it, the better. If you want to unsubscribe from my email distributions, please inform me.

The Revised First Edition (RFE) will be available at Amazon this week—my best guess is by 11/29/17. The price is $21.95. *What a great investment you'll make if you buy it!* I'll refer to the RFE page numbers in future emails.

The RFE incorporates three changes:

1. Typos found—less than a dozen of them—have been corrected. If you find a typo(s), please let me know.

2. Changes have been made to add clarity. If you see the need for more of this type of change, please let me know.

3. Appendices G and H are new. Appendix G includes the G&P Orientation as well as the four emails (which include this one) that I've sent in November 2017. Less than 100 copies of the original 135-page book (published October 16, 2016) have been sold or given away. I strongly urge you to buy a copy of the RFE (151 pages). If you already have what is now the "old" edition of the book, I'll reimburse the $19.95 you spent on it—upon request.

Regards,

John

6. An Email Indicating the Enthusiasm of a Retired Minister of Music

Sent: Sunday, November 19, 2017 1:28 AM
Subject: The Grow-and-Protect Investment Strategy Book

John,

Your recent email was a welcome surprise! It's been way too long since we've had a face-to-face conversation.

We ordered your book via Amazon Prime just a few days ago and it arrived a day or two ago. My wife, a retired minister of music, read Chapters 6 & 7 yesterday and was so enthused about it that I read them this morning!

As soon as practical, we will be ordering 4 more copies of your book: 1 for each one of our 3 children and one for a xfriend recently retired from the University of Tulsa where he was involved with the KWGS radio station. If it is at all possible, we would like for you to autograph these 4 copies.

Perhaps we can renew our dialogue via email & texting; eyeball to eyeball conversations are my preference.

It was a joy this morning discovering my recollections of previous dialogues as I was reading Chapters 6 and 7 of your book. It was at your first "God and the Stock Market" class in August 1997 [p. 70, second bullet point] that we first met.

Do you still fish?

A comment of note: Our older son has a copy of your previous book. He is presently supervising our portfolios as we attempt to get our estate in tip-top-shape while we transition thru our aging process!

Best regards,

Nelson

Appendix H

◇◇◇◇◇◇◇◇◇◇◇◇◇

The Big Takeaway from Analyzing Table 3-2

The bottom line in Table 3-2 (p. 41)—for the 50-year period 1966–2015—shows impressive performance statistics. The **G&P** model had a mean annual return of 16% versus 11% for **B&H**. Due to rounding to the nearest full percent to make Table 3-2 as user-friendly as possible, the difference is 6%, not 5%. Column (6) reveals that the mean wealth self-insurance paid under the **G&P** model for the 14 years it occurred was 3%. That's low-cost portfolio insurance!

While those findings are impressive indeed, this Appendix provides the big takeaway from analyzing Table 3-2. Using the year-by-year data from Table 3-2, this analysis involves classifying the 50 years in four categories: Type 1 years, Type 2 years, Type 3 years and Type 4 years.

Type 1 Years (n = 8)

Definition: **G&P** annual return is equal to **B&H** annual return (that is, there were no **G&P** trades). Typically, these years were bullish.

Type 1 Years	Number of Trades	G&P Return	B&H Return (S&P 500)	Difference in Return
1975	0	37%	37%	0%
1976	0	24%	24%	0%
1983	0	23%	23%	0%
1986	0	18%	18%	0%
1988	0	17%	17%	0%
1993	0	10%	10%	0%
1995	0	37%	37%	0%
1997	0	33%	33%	0%
Mean	0	25%	25%	0%

Type 2 Years (n = 15)

Definition: "Wealth self-insurance" [pp. 36, 40–41 column (6) and p. 43] was paid in the sense that money was lost due to trading. Typically, these years were bullish.

Type 2 Years	Number of Trades	G&P Return	B&H Return (S&P 500)	Difference in Return
1971	8	13%	14%	−1%
1972	6	14%	19%	−5%
1979	5	17%	18%	−1%
1985	2	28%	32%	−4%
1989	2	28%	31%	−3%
1991	2	28%	31%	−3%
1992	2	2%	8%	−6%
1994	8	−1%	1%	−2%
1996	2	21%	23%	−2%
1999	6	20%	21%	−1%
2005	4	3%	5%	−2%
2006	2	12%	16%	−3%*
2010	4	12%	15%	−3%
2012	6	6%	16%	−10%
2013	6	31%	32%	−2%
Mean	4	16%	19%	−3%

*Note: It appears this figure should be −4%; however, it is −3% due to rounding. In the remainder of this Appendix there are several other cases of such rounding error, but they aren't marked.

Type 3 Years (n = 10)

Definition: No wealth self-insurance was paid because, in these bullish years, G&P return exceeded B&H return due to trading.

Type 3 Years	Number of Trades	G&P Return	B&H Return (S&P 500)	Difference in Return
1967	2	26%	24%	2%
1968	2	12%	11%	0%
1978	5	10%	7%	3%
1980	4	41%	32%	9%
1984	4	7%	6%	1%
2003	2	31%	29%	2%
2004	2	12%	11%	1%
2007	7	6%	5%	0%
2014	3	15%	14%	1%
2015	10	5%	1%	3%
Mean	4	17%	13%	4%

Type 4 Years (n = 17)

Definition: The same years that are shaded in Table 3-2 (pp. 40–41); in these bearish years—that is, bearish during at least part of the year—G&P return exceeded B&H return due to trading.[1]

Type 4 Years	Number of Trades	G&P Return	B&H Return (S&P 500)	Difference in Return
1966	12	4%	−10%	14%
1969	10	−1%	−9%	7%
1970	6	34%	4%	30%
1973	12	3%	−15%	18%
1974	14	−5%	−26%	21%
1977	4	−1%	−7%	7%
1981	2	−3%	−5%	2%
1982	6	30%	21%	8%
1987	6	26%	5%	21%
1990	10	3%	−3%	6%
1998	10	34%	29%	5%
2000	5	−4%	−9%	5%
2001	3	6%	−12%	18%
2002	4	2%	−22%	24%
2008	13	4%	−37%	41%
2009	2	52%	26%	26%
2011	6	8%	2%	6%
Mean	7	11%	−4%	15%

The tabulation of the bottom lines—the findings—for each type of year above are as follows:

Classification (1)	Number of Years (2)	Number of Trades (3)	Mean G&P Return (4)	B&H Return (S&P 500) (5)	Difference in Return (6)
Type 1 years	8	0	25%	25%	0%
Type 2 years	14	4	16%	19%	−3%
Type 3 years	11	4	16%	14%	2%
Type 4 years	17	7	11%	−4%	15%
Total	50				
Mean weighted by years		4.4	16%	11%	5%

Note that the bottom line for columns (3) and (6) differ slightly from the bottom line of Table 3-2 due to rounding error.

---

1   For example, consider 1998. For the year as a whole, the S&P 500 return was 28.6%. But for the period 07/17/98 to 08/31/98, the S&P 500 fell 19.3%. That steep decline meets my own criterion of a bear market, −19%, slightly different than Wall Street's criterion of −20%. I prefer −19% because there were five "bear markets" during 1966–2015 that had declines between 19.0% and 19.9%.

A very important finding from this tabulation is the outstanding returns for the 17 Type 4 years. The mean annual return for those years was 11% for the G&P model vs. −4% for B&H. That difference of 15% is spectacular!

Moreover, every Type 4 year had a G&P return that was greater than the B&H return by at least 5%, with one minor exception (1981). Although five of these years had a negative G&P return (ranging from −1% to −5%), B&H had larger negative returns in those years:

Year	G&P Return	B&H Return
1969	−1%	−9%
1974	−5%	−26%
1977	−2%	−7%
1981	−3%	−5%
2000	−4%	−9%

In 2008, another Type 4 year, G&P return was 0%, and B&H return was −37.0%. Wow!

Note that the first email distribution of each new calendar year will report on the G&P model's and B&H's returns for the year just completed. The email at the beginning of 2018 will include the returns for both 2016 and 2017—to update Table 3-2 (p. 41).

GLOSSARY

◇◇◇◇◇◇◇◇◇◇◇◇◇◇◇◇◇◇

The Glossary is the Important Terms to Know, which are in boldface when they first appear in this book.

Actively-managed mutual funds. These funds are managed by professional money managers who engage in stock picking or market timing in an effort to outperform a benchmark index such as the S&P 500. A main reason these funds have a tendency to underperform the S&P 500 is high management fees. (p. 17)

Asset allocation. Deciding on and maintaining a suitable mix of asset classes in your portfolio as you move through the seasons of life. Your portfolio is the total of your 401(k) [403(b), 457 or Thrift Savings Plan], IRA and taxable accounts. (p. 23 and p. 83)

Asset classes. They include (1) domestic stocks, (2) foreign stocks, (3) real estate investment trusts (REITs), (4) bonds and (5) cash equivalents. (p. 84)

Behavioral finance. The field of study that pictures a world in which investment decisions are far more complex than modern portfolio theory's cold tradeoffs that weigh only numerical measures of risk and return. It recognizes the influence that human emotions and reactions—hopes of earning great profits, fear of difficult choices and inconsistent reasoning about money—exert in economic and investment decisions. (p. 93)

Buy-and-hold (B&H) strategy. The strategy of simply buying-and-holding an asset class. The focus of this book is using the B&H strategy for the S&P 500. (p. 13)

Cyclically adjusted price/earnings (CAPE) ratio. Developed by Robert Shiller, a Nobel Prize winning economist, this ratio is based on the S&P 500's current price divided by its average earnings over the past 10 years adjusted for inflation. Compared to the traditional price-earnings ratio, CAPE is a less volatile valuation indicator. (p. 55, pp. 107–108)

Data mining. The process of searching historical data for patterns that repeat themselves with a high degree of consistency. This process is facilitated by computing power becoming so inexpensive and is the basis of both the B&H strategy and the G&P strategy. (p. 13)

Dividend yield (see **S&P 500's dividend yield**).

Dollar-cost averaging. The systematic approach of investing a set amount of money at regular intervals, such as making monthly contributions to your 401(k). (p. 14)

Efficient market theory (EMT). This theory maintains that prices in the financial markets fully incorporate all known information. As a result, market prices change only in response to new information, which is called news. Under this theory, any attempt at market timing is considered to be a fool's errand. That's because past stock prices are generally thought to be a completely unreliable source for forecasting future stock prices in any way that would outperform the B&H strategy, when risk is taken into account. (p. 22)

Exchange-rate risk. This risk results from fluctuations in the value of foreign currencies in relation to the value of the U.S. dollar. (p. 86)

Exchange-traded funds (ETFs). These funds trade all day like stocks. The G&P strategy uses low-cost S&P 500 ETFs for market timing; three of them are listed in the bottom section of Table 1-3, p. 16. (p. 15)

Favorable season. This season is November 1st through April 30th. Beginning November 1, 1960 and ending April 30, 2016, an investment in the S&P 500 only during this season would have grown about 63-fold. (p. 109)

Financial market anomaly. The notion that any investment strategy that, over a long period, generated abnormal returns—returns which, after taking risk into account, exceeded the market's mean return for that long period. (p. 50)

G&P strategy's annual return. The sum of the S&P 500's price change and the companies' cash dividends paid to investors (the dividend yield), expressed as a percentage of its beginning-of-the-year price. (p. 39)

G&P strategy's risk. The uncertainty of the future market value of the asset held—the S&P 500 or cash. In the practical application of this definition of risk, investors mainly concern themselves with the possibility of the market value declining. There are two simple but useful measures of the G&P strategy's risk: (1) its annual declines and (2) the minimum number of calendar years needed to avoid a loss. (p. 45)

Good and Bad Times (GBT) model. Appendix F explains this model in detail. (pp. 123–130)

Grow-and-Protect (G&P) strategy. This market-timing strategy attempts to "Sell, then buy lower." Specifically, that means selling a low-cost S&P 500 ETF and trying to buy it back at a lower price. Historically, a buy or sell signal has occurred, on average, about once every 2½ months. The time the traffic signal is red accounts for all of the difference in performance between the B&H strategy and the G&P strategy. (p. 37)

Hulbert Financial Digest (HFD). This ground-breaking newsletter, launched in 1980, tracked the performance of investment newsletters. Mark Hulbert's tracking research spoke volumes about the quality, or lack thereof, of newsletters and was a severe test for portfolio managers. HFD shut down in March 2016. (p. 28)

Inflation. The decline in the purchasing power of a monetary unit, such as the U.S. dollar. (p. 86)

Longevity risk. The unpleasant possibility of you (you and your spouse) outliving your wealth. (p. 23 and p. 87)

Low-cost S&P 500 index funds. A number of these funds are listed in Table 1-3, p. 16.

Market risk. The extent to which an investment's value is subject to fluctuation. The greater the possible fluctuations in market value, the greater the investment's market risk. (p. 85)

Modern portfolio theory (MPT). This theory's early development boils down to two main tenets: (1) asset allocation and (2) the efficient market theory (EMT). (p. 21)

My life-changing spiritual experience. This experience occurred on the evening of July 20, 1997 (pp. 66–67).

Rebalancing. This activity restores a portfolio to the investor's desired asset allocation. The restoration increases the portfolio's return while decreasing its risk. An easy way to remember to rebalance annually is to do it on or near your birthday. (p. 89)

Refined January Barometer. The S&P 500's January change as a predictor of its change for the remaining 11 months of the year. (p. 111)

Reversion to the mean. An immutable force affecting the S&P 500 (and at work in all financial markets). Under this force, periods of high returns tend to occur after periods of lower returns, and in turn, periods of low returns tend to follow periods of higher returns. (p. 12)

S&P 500. The broad-based large company index that comprises about 80% of the total market value of all publicly traded U.S. stocks and some 40% of the total market value of all publicly traded stocks in the entire world. The S&P 500 is embedded in the culture such that some investors think a lot about its movements, even while on vacation. (p. 3)

S&P 500's annual return. The sum of its price change and the companies' cash dividends paid (reinvested dividends or dividend yield), expressed as a percentage of its beginning-of-the-year price. (p. 6)

S&P 500's dividend yield. The 500 companies' cash dividends paid to investors, expressed as a percentage of its beginning-of-the-year price. For 1966–2015, the S&P 500's dividend yield ranged from 1.04% for 2000 to 6.65% for 1982. (p. 6)

S&P 500 index funds. These funds are passively-managed so they mimic the S&P 500's return. There are two types of index funds: mutual funds and exchange-traded funds (ETFs). (p. 15)

S&P 500's risk. The uncertainty of its future market value. In the practical application of this definition of risk, investors mainly concern themselves with the possibility of the S&P 500 declining in market value. There are two simple but useful measures of the S&P 500's risk: (1) its largest declines and (2) the minimum number of calendar years needed to avoid a loss. (p. 9)

Target-date fund. The type of fund, known by names such as freedom fund and target retirement fund, automatically adjusts the investor's asset allocation as the year she plans to retire approaches and is surpassed, to take into account her diminishing tolerance for the risk of investing in stocks. This type of fund is a convenient, albeit generally expensive, way to achieve suitable asset allocation through the seasons of life. (p. 90)

Technical analysis. This analysis uses data generated by the stock market itself or data from any other source to forecast the stock market (in this book, to forecast the S&P 500). (p. 51)

TIAA Real Estate Fund. One of the funds that are the core of the TIAA-CREF retirement program for employees of universities and some not-for-profit organizations. (p. 112)

Time horizon. An estimate of how many years there will be from today through the last time you (you and your spouse) withdraw money from your portfolio for living expenses. (p. 87)

Tolerance for risk. The combination of the investor's willingness to take risk and her ability to prudently take risk. Tolerance for risk tends to be difficult to estimate. (p. 88)

Unfavorable season. This season is May 1st through October 31st. Beginning May 1, 1961 and ending October 31, 2015, an investment in the S&P 500 only for this season would have grown about 2-fold. (p. 109)

Value Line's Median Appreciation Potential (MAP). On a weekly basis, Value Line forecasts the appreciation potential for each of the some 1,700 stocks it follows. The MAP is the forecast for the stock that ranks 850th in appreciation potential. (p. 112)

Volatility Index (VIX). This is often referred to as the "fear index." In this context, fear refers to concern regarding the near-term possibility of a sizable decline in the S&P 500. If fear is low, the VIX is low; if fear is high, the VIX is high. (p. 108)

Wealth self-insurance. For 1966–2015 (50 years), the G&P investor would have paid wealth self-insurance in the 14 years when G&P underperformed B&H—for all cases during bull markets; in those years, the mean annual cost of this insurance was 3% of the G&P strategy's portion of the investor's portfolio. (p. 36) This concept is introduced on p. 36; it appears in column (6) of Table 3-2, pp. 40–41; and is discussed on p. 43.

CPSIA information can be obtained
at www.ICGtesting.com
Printed in the USA
BVOW11s1540200218
508514BV00009BBA/104/P